HELLO TRAUMA

DR. HILLARY CAUTHEN

Mental Performance Advantage, LLC | Pflugerville, Texas

Published by
Mental Performance Advantage, LLC | Pflugerville, Texas

Publisher's Cataloging-in-Publication Data
Cauthen, Hillary.

Hello trauma : our invisible teammate / Hillary Cauthen. –
Pflugerville, TX : Mental Performance Advantage, LLC, 2023.

p. ; cm.

ISBN13: 978-0-9601219-0-8

1. Psychic trauma. 2. Mental healing. I. Title.

BF175.5.P75 C38 2023
155.93--dc23

Project coordination by Jenkins Group, Inc. | www.jenkinsgroupinc.com

Front cover design by T. Dewayne Johnson
Interior design by Brooke Camfield

Printed in the United States of America
27 26 25 24 23 • 5 4 3 2 1

CONTENTS

Hello Trauma
Our Invisible Teammate

Note to the Reader:

The following journal entries are a work of fiction and do not depict any specific person or their personal experiences. They are intended to represent a culmination of the emotions, struggles, and healing processes that individuals who have experienced trauma may go through. While the entries aim to provide a general understanding of the journey faced by trauma survivors, they should not be considered as accurate representations of any specific individual's story. The purpose of these journal entries is to create empathy and awareness regarding the challenges faced by those who have experienced trauma. They explore common themes, reactions, and coping mechanisms that individuals may encounter during their healing process. However, it is important to recognize that each person's experience of trauma is unique, and no single narrative can fully encompass the diverse range of responses and recovery paths.

INTRODUCTION

It's been resolved.

For anyone who has experienced trauma, these words have deep meaning. But they don't mean what they sound like. What if *it* is so big and destructive that two letters can never capture what *it* is and what it did to someone's well-being and sense of safety? And *been*, in the past tense, all cleaned up, nothing to see here, folks. Finally, *resolved*, as though the issue has been neatly packaged up, put away, and relegated to the past, totally forgotten and managed. It's been dealt with and handled.

But for who? Not for the person who experienced the trauma that led to *resolution*. Rarely has anything been resolved. It hasn't been cleaned up, or even closed off, disconnected from their feelings and how they live in the world in trauma's aftermath. This is not in the past tense or a distant memory collecting dust as part of someone's experience and history on earth. *It* is very much in the present, and resolution is not always accessible to people who have been harmed and traumatized.

These three words—just fifteen letters—are all around us, but they require closer examination. They're a smoke screen intended to conceal, and they leave many people trapped in their intended silence.

This is what trauma is and what it does: It takes our voices away. It hijacks our minds. It leaves people feeling alone and scared. It's ugly and it's everywhere, though we don't often address it, because it's hard to look closely at it. We may not see it as clearly as we should, but we need to learn how to identify it, how to understand it, and how to heal from it. The reason this is so important is simple: trauma is on every team, in every office, in every family and every community. It's a part of human experience, and it isn't something we can pretend isn't part of our lives, and all around us.

Trauma can be our worst enemy, controlling every play in our lives. Or it can be a teammate we can learn to understand, so we can use its strength and everything it can teach us. It gives us a chance to build and grow with it so we can become the champions of our own lives. We can put the energy into working with it, or we can let it go unexamined, which means we're working against it, but it's still there and can never be fully resolved without our care and attention. Even if the trauma isn't ours but is impacting someone close to us, we all end up carrying the weight. Learning to work with and understand someone, their pain, and their emotional challenges is everyone's responsibility, because trauma is so common and shows up on every team.

Trauma is like an invisible scar just under the skin that victims can feel, but others can't usually see. Even victims themselves aren't always sure it's there, but once it is, it makes itself at home in our bodies, minds, and hearts. It's stored in our nervous system, releasing anxiety, shame, anger, and sadness, and it leaves sufferers on high alert, in a state of reactivity, even when they don't know why they feel the way they do.

This is a story of healing, a quest to take action that protects people, and a hope to resolve the unresolvable. It's for your healing, my healing, and everyone trying to work through how trauma has affected their life. Trauma leaves so many people struggling to find *their* words, find *their* voices, and communicate *their* feelings through the most painful confusion. We're all trying to figure out how to live again, and most of us don't have the help we need. We don't have the language, we don't trust anyone or anything, and we feel lost.

There is life after trauma, and finding a way out of this silence is required for healing to begin. Until we can understand and talk about our trauma, though, we remain in the holding pattern of being sad, hurt, anxious, and sick. We're going through the motions, with our internal scar fighting for our attention at all times.

Trauma that is left untreated, unprocessed, or unexamined doesn't go away on its own. The symptoms may diminish over time, but the shards remain buried as triggers, cutting through our day to day lives, dimming our light, and changing us. Trauma creates a new blueprint for our minds, in which a sense of danger lurks all around us, even after the threat is long gone. We know it when we feel it—even when we're not sure where it's coming from—and many of us live with this chronic discomfort every day.

The health impacts from unresolved trauma put people at increased risk for mental health diagnoses and a long list of physical health problems. Some people, if not all, may experience unexpressed anger, flashbacks and intrusive memories, sleep disturbances, eating disorders, anxiety, and panic attacks; living in a state of being on high alert may become the new norm. High blood pressure, strokes, heart attacks, and depression may follow from the stress trauma can produce. Post-traumatic stress disorder (PTSD) is a real and common consequence. The symptoms don't always show up immediately but can surface years later as a normal human response to horrible experiences we have buried to protect ourselves.

This is why it's so important that we truly accept and try to understand the trauma in our lives. Pretending it's not there is not the answer. Ignoring it keeps it alive. Recovery is possible once we process traumatic memories, releasing them from being trapped inside us. It is only when we are able to reintegrate a traumatic memory or experience into our mind and the rest of our lives that our brains can begin to heal. We deserve to heal, and we can.

There is life, and more love, and more peace, calm, and *actual* resolution when we show ourselves the care we need as we recover from trauma. No one can do this for us, even if they tell us *it's been resolved*. *We* are in control of our own personal healing, growth, and resolution, no one else. Certainly not the people who tell us *they're* over it, or *they* "resolved" the situation, or *they* think it's been put away and forgotten. It's not up to them, it's up to us.

ONE

Hello Trauma

Hello, Trauma.

It's been 2 days.

I can't breathe, and I can't speak.

Silence sends my mind racing and my heart pounding in my chest, shooting stress through my body, bathing me in anxiety. There are moments when I don't understand what happened, but I feel fear all around me, and I can't catch my breath. Language fails me, leaving me alone in my head. I want to scream, run, and weep, but even that only feels like a moment of relief. I can't get comfortable. My body is on fire from the anxiety. Every sense is in overdrive, and my brain can't keep up. I can barely remember my own name. It's so crowded in there.

Screaming, crying, and running away don't change much of anything for me. How will I ever get this out of me? I want to snap my fingers to change the world, so no one ever feels this way again. I'm so hurt and angry that people need to be protected from harm, but we need protection in the most urgent way. Is that even possible in my current state? How can I ever feel safe again?

Putting a thought together—never mind a sentence—is so much harder than it used to be because right under the surface is the boiling mess of trauma I carry. I can scream in my own head, but what good is that doing? It only hurts me. I feel trapped that trying to talk about this, asking for help, seeking support, or beginning to understand it consumes me. This feels too big to even talk about. How can I put an entire horrible experience into one word? Something that captures every nuance, nightmare, shock of adrenaline, every tear, sleepless night, anxious day, or moment of time lost to this?

I can't breathe and I can't speak. All I do is sit and think.

Sam

* * *

Trauma.

It's such a huge word, we barely understand it. Can these awful feelings, this painful state of "living" be captured in words and communicated? Can the enormous complexity of a terrible, negative experience be explained? We hear it so often, we barely think about what it means, or acknowledge its scale. It seems simple enough: it's an experience that produces psychological injury or pain, though it's different for every victim.

This psychological misery is enormous territory. We've taken the power away from what it means to have trauma, and are desensitized by how common it is, because we forget how much pain it's caused us. We look away from it. We hide from it. Subconsciously, we start to think that we should just get over it, that we're inadequate or weak if we're still feeling it. We hurry ourselves to forget and move on, rather than actively do the work to heal it.

Trauma is heavy and hard to carry, and more often than not, it's difficult for us to see it in other people. But it's there, and it needs attention. In fact, it's everywhere.

This word brings shame, judgment, confusion, misery, and pain. "Trauma" packs a punch. It heightens fear, increases our default state of irritation, and leads to chronic stress. It makes it hard to calm and soothe ourselves and keeps us reactive. It traps us in survival mode, directing all our mental and physical energy toward dealing with a threat. It desensitizes us by keeping us stuck.

Trauma tricks us. It's as though our brains become hostage to an event in our lives. It can suppress our memory and impulse control and trap a person in a constant state of strong emotional reactivity, like hypervigilance. Just living with trauma becomes like running a marathon, every day. It can affect our hormones, making us more sensitive to stressors, and we're not built to live with constant threats.

Making matters worse, trauma disrupts the function that enables us to distinguish between the past and the present, let alone to begin seeing or hoping for things in the future. Trauma robs us of the ability to tell the difference between an actual traumatic event and our memories of it. Trauma is persistent and is always working for our attention. It does not give up. And it doesn't go away until we face it.

After we experience trauma, it can take a while to make sense of the words in our head, as they echo and bounce around and get louder. Being in a state of shock, we can't make sense of what we're thinking, we can't decode the noise, as shock numbs us. We've all experienced shock. It's physical as much as it's psychological. It's a critical condition brought on by a sudden drop of blood flow through the body, and it depletes every resource we have. Shock sends our body into a dangerous fight for survival, and the weak, rapid pulse, dizziness, nausea, and surge of stress hormones leave a path of destruction in their wake. Depending on the severity of the circumstances, these physiological symptoms may dissipate on their own in minutes, or may last much, much longer, leading to acute stress disorder or PTSD.

Shock can come from something as small as a bee sting for some people, or from something as big and complex as trauma. It can be physically violent or psychologically abusive. It can be chronic and repeated, or one event that changes who we are. It can be a car wreck, a war, an assault, a loss, or virtually anything else that destroys our sense of safety. But the result is the same: when a person is in shock, functioning at even the lowest level is virtually impossible.

People that experience shock are awash in intense stress reactions. Their breathing, blood pressure, and heart rate increase, their muscles tighten, and their entire system gets ready to fight, flee, freeze, or even fawn. In terms of trauma responses, fighting and confronting a threat results in anger, rage, high energy, and action. Flight—running away from a threat—causes anxiety, panic, avoidance, and a surge in adrenaline. Freezing causes us to shut down to block out the threat, which leads to numbness, dissociation, and low energy. But fawning makes us appease the threat, leading to people-pleasing, codependency, and an unhealthy lack of boundaries.

Fawning means consistently abandoning our own needs to serve others, keep the peace, and get along, and trauma is often at the root of the fawn response. We do this to try and re-establish a sense of safety. It's much like a coping mechanism that survivors of complex trauma adopt, at the expense of their own needs, to calm their abuser, diffuse scary situations, and feel safe. This represses natural and healthy expressions of anger or fear and doesn't allow the emotion to move from inside the body toward something outside the self, which is how the fight or flight response was designed to work. It leaves fawners stuck, drowning in repressed anger, as the rage, fear, and disgust stay in the body indefinitely.

When our bodies recognize a threat and enter into a trauma response, cortisol, the primary stress hormone, floods the system and couples with adrenaline, which is there to get us moving. Both hormones are messengers crucial for our survival. They scream: *Respond and react. You are in trouble. You are not safe.*

When we can't leave a threat behind because it's woven into our environment, we're forced to live with it, which deepens the trauma. Anxiety becomes our constant companion. When we can't talk about what's happening and how we're feeling, the anxiety only worsens. And it's hard to talk about, for nearly everyone, because so many people feel that no one really wants to hear how terrible an experience was. It leaves victims struggling to make themselves understood. This kind of silence only makes everything worse.

The tragedy of trauma is that so many people experience it, but we're rarely able to connect with one another about it and really share our true feelings. This makes trauma very difficult to heal from. It's there to protect us, but it can also teach us about our own safety. Trauma is the way our brains and bodies adapt to an experience or an environment of life-threatening powerlessness, from a single moment of terror to an ongoing experience of fear. Trauma is the story of emotion and thought trapped in our body in survival mode, triggered from an external force. This event imprints in our mind to protect us. Trauma sticks around to remind us of what can happen in our lives.

When we ignore our trauma and repress the natural and healthy responses to fear and danger, it can lead to loneliness, isolation, pent up anger, and leave us producing too much cortisol, our primary stress hormone. Chronically high cortisol levels can cause persistent high blood sugar, diabetes, anxiety, depression, chronic exhaustion, headaches, stomach issues, heart disease, and high blood pressure.

Goodness, trauma sucks. It creates a disaster for the human body and mind, regardless of whether we fight, flee, freeze, or fawn. No matter how we handle it, it leaves us in a dangerous and weakened physiological state, which is why it's so important that we learn how to handle and process the pain trauma causes. Because even if we're not aware that we're carrying traumatic experiences with us, our bodies know and are trying to handle the stress of protecting ourselves.

Everyone responds to traumatic experiences differently, but the goal is the same: to protect ourselves and minimize any more pain to our mental, physical, and emotional well-being. What we miss by wearing this armor of protection, though, is the ability to listen to what's going on inside us that needs to heal. We miss the gift of awareness in our instant state of shock.

We're consumed and caught up in our protective responses. We don't listen to the screaming voices in our head. We don't want to acknowledge the pain we are in. But there comes a time when the protective gear gets too heavy to wear, and we have to take it off.

The moment we strip away the weight of the trauma and look within to see the emotional mess we've hidden, it can unleash raw, vulnerable, enormously messy emotions. Feelings of anger, denial, fear, shame, confusion, and complete powerlessness can consume the space we occupy in the world. No one can live this way forever, though, so many of us try to hide this pain for far too long. To heal, to function fully, we must force ourselves to examine the pain, as hard as that can be.

Only during this process of awareness and actualization can we find our power over what has hurt us so deeply. This power is different for each person, but it's driven by passion, a commitment to the self, to fight for yourself sometimes *against* yourself—since examining pain can cause more pain—to fight the emotional war in our head, and finally to defeat the trauma.

But let's be clear: fighting is not without pain. It hurts in ways we can't anticipate, because we have no idea how hard the other side will fight back. We don't know what fighting ourselves and our own feelings will mean or how hard it might be. We don't know what's coming, what form it will take, or how long the fight will last. But trauma requires a response of *some* kind, and at least fighting feels like some kind of action.

Victims often experience three versions of themselves when they suffer from a traumatic event. I define these versions of self as the *Minimizer*, the *Enabler*, and the *Moral Authority*. Victims will oscillate between these versions of themselves while a traumatic event is occurring, when making sense of the event(s) if there is recurring trauma, and later, when reflecting on the past traumatic experience. In moments of intense stress and fear, we split into parts in order to protect ourselves.

The *Minimizer* is in denial, downplaying the experience in an effort to make it feel less impactful and harmful, as though it's not destroying us. This is a version of "freeze," in which denied feelings are less painful because we aren't really experiencing them in the moment, and when traumatic events are happening, we're driven by fear. The *Minimizer* will also show up in reflective periods when naming or discussing the traumatic event. The *Minimizer* decreases the relevance of the experience and forces the mind to tell us it's not as bad as someone else's experience. This version of self is trying to protect our emotional well-being by denying the impact of the pain, by ignoring the fear produced in the event. However, this sense of self results in ignoring the overwhelming and often life-altering significance of the experience and our needs and reinforces living in a state of numbness and fear.

Fear is the awareness of danger. It starts in the brain's amygdala, which responds to threats like the sight of a predator, so we get ready to move. Fear played an important role in our evolution and survival, and it's necessary for our safety even today. But it's such a visceral reaction—honed throughout human history—that regardless of where the stimulation comes from, it immediately changes our chemistry. We may not be able to push past fear in a conscious, deliberate way, but what happens to us psychologically is automatic, and leaves us feeling drained. No matter the cause, our physiological response to fear is built to be intense. We don't forget it.

When we experience trauma and initially deny its impact, the *Minimizer* is activated, protecting us from naming ourselves a victim, preventing us from consciously admitting it's real. This state of trauma response is powerful, terrifying, and potentially life-threatening.

Next, a logical version of us emerges, the *Enabler*. This formation of the self tries to make meaning from our experiences, leaning into our empathetic nature and exploring why someone would do something to harm us. We begin to look within ourselves to search for what it was that we did to cause this trauma to happen. We may develop an emotional engagement with and attachment to the perpetrator or event that's causing us so much stress and anxiety, yet our sense of self is trying to rationalize and take responsibility for the traumatic event.

The *Enabler* often emerges during the event and more often when reflecting upon how and why this traumatic event could and did occur. The *Enabler* is taking ownership of the trauma, punishing oneself more than the perpetrator could, telling us we are at fault for what's happening. The *Enabler* is confusing, emotionally hijacking our logical meaning-making processor of events and causes us to get stuck in our healing process.

Finally, the hero version of ourselves emerges, the *Moral Authority*, which aims to take care of us. This formation of self is like an outsider looking in, working to help us make meaning of the events we're experiencing, confirming that the harm done to us was wrong, and that we are justifiably hurt. The *Moral Authority* removes the emotional confusion we have been suffering in and awakens the self to begin healing. This version of ourselves helps us to admit that, yes, something bad happened, yes, we have been suffering, yes, we are a victim, and, yes, what occurred was wrong. The *Moral Authority* validates the emotional pain we're in, confirms that action needs to be taken, that we are not responsible for the pain we experience. Finding the *Moral Authority* is the start of getting angry, fueling the self to find ourselves, to heal, and to live.

* * *

Hello, Trauma,

It's been 9 days.

I've barely gotten out of bed. I can't remember the last time I ate, slept, or left the house. I haven't been able to speak to anyone. I don't know what day it is, what time it is, and I can't remember where I'm supposed to be. Don't I have responsibilities? Who cares, I can barely function. It doesn't matter anyway, since I have nothing to offer at the moment.

Maybe they'll notice I'm gone, maybe they won't. I don't care. Just breathing right now is harder than I can manage, so nothing else matters. The idea of standing up for myself is so exhausting, I can't even imagine. But aren't I supposed to? Am I doing this wrong? No one can help me if I can't ask, and I can't speak. Maybe tomorrow I'll find the strength to fight. Maybe.

Peter

* * *

TWO

Hello Confusion

Hello, Trauma,

Day 5 here. Why is this happening?

Bottomless thoughts are swirling through my head, and I don't want to hear them. There's a word that doesn't belong to me: victim. Or does it? Am I now a victim? Am I a victim if I didn't speak up sooner? Am I a victim if I took steps to stop what was happening, and no one listened? How did I get here? How did this happen?

What does it mean to be a victim? I've never thought of myself this way.

How could no one hear me asking for help, for intervention, for support? Did my own insecurities and false confidence lead them to believe I was okay? I'm forcing myself to make it look as though I have it under control. It's virtually impossible to do this, when the control belongs to other people, but I'm trying with everything I have. I'm failing.

Get into your car, walk into your home, hold it in until you can fall apart there. Look in the mirror. Try to recognize yourself behind the tears. You don't have it under control. What a joke. You're really falling to pieces under the surface. You can take the mask off alone at home where no one can see, but when you leave the house, force the smile back onto your face. Pull it together. Come on. You can do it. You can't be a victim out in the world, hold it together. Only at home can you be safe, where no one can see you.

Robbie

* * *

According to the National Alliance on Mental Illness, it's estimated that 70 percent of adults in the United States have experienced a traumatic event at least once in their lives. Chances are this number underreports how much trauma we're living with. Up to 20 percent of these victims go on to develop PTSD. In any given year, an estimated eight million adults are struggling with PTSD in the United States, and many more are trying to deal with trauma, often with no help.

Let that sink in: 70 percent of adults around us. Beyond trauma occurring frequently, the fact that we ignore it makes it so much worse. The reality is, we don't know how to deal with so much trauma, which keeps it buried and hidden. We're unskilled at seeing and hearing it, and we aren't paying attention to the right things. We don't prioritize the pain that's right in front of us, all around us, and in us. We don't support our fundamental human needs like connection, psychological safety and security, transparency, and trust, and all of this affects our ability to deal with and process traumatic events.

Put another way, trauma is not only more common than we think, it's actually the norm, varying in degrees, but affecting nearly everyone, whether they know it or not. And even if an individual isn't traumatized themselves, they're connected to people who are. Trauma affects their relationships, connections, and how empathy and compassion are accessible in their lives, which means that trauma is impacting *every* interaction on one level or another.

It's not that some people—those who have been traumatized—are weak or pathological, and the few who are untraumatized around us are strong and normal. It's that most people are suffering and there are more traumatic events than we can possibly imagine. These don't have to be *dramatic* events that make headlines and are honored on anniversaries. Instead, most traumas occur quietly behind closed doors, hidden from view of anyone but the person or people left damaged.

In some instances, trauma is so common, we don't even label it trauma because our traumatic experiences have socialized us to think it's the norm, and victims minimize the experience of it. They just take it because it's part of life. But even these moments of micro traumas build and encode in our memories. Our brain learns to react and respond differently in these settings, normalizing what is not normal. We live this way so often, leaning into our internal *Minimizer* as we adapt and change ourselves, instead of recognizing that traumatic things are happening. Instead of pushing for change in our environments, we just absorb the problem.

We don't talk about this. We're ashamed, scared, disgusted and we deny trauma is even happening, as though collectively, we're trying to protect ourselves from the reality of our situation, which can be really hard to take. We maintain the status quo because it's easier than changing. There's no doubt that changing is hard work. But it's not only possible, it's necessary so we can address all this trauma.

To look critically at how much trauma there is around us would require us to understand it, see how much needs to change, and then figure out how to change it. Psychologically, this would create a ton of fear, and fear is really unpleasant to live in constantly. But sufferers of trauma are *already* afraid all the time. This is why we need to fight for change. We owe a debt to every victim of trauma in every environment, because people are being silenced and are exhausted from living this way.

Don't get me wrong, I am not here to label every bad, negative interaction as trauma. I'm also not living in a false reality that the world will be rainbows and butterflies where we eat ice cream all day and dance in the sunshine—although that does sound nice. I'm here to say something practical and actionable so we can help millions of people heal. Let's code a common language around trauma, and actually assist in preventative care, accountable actions, and care for others. Change—cultural change—is needed to minimize the impact of trauma or minimize the opportunity for trauma to occur. For this to happen, we need to work at it.

But *what* exactly do we need to change? Apathy. Indifference. Believing we're powerless. Victim shaming and blaming. Being passive bystanders when we know something is wrong. Looking the other way when something destructive is happening right in front of us. We need to change how hard we look *for* and *at* trauma, even though when we begin looking hard, we will see trauma nearly everywhere. Yes, this is uncomfortable, and it's painful. We will want to stop trying to make change. But our epidemic of untreated trauma requires that we work together on this.

Our default setting of "That is not my problem" is making millions of people sick and leaving too many people stuck in silent pain. It's *everyone's* problem, which means we all can play a role in making this positive change. We need to fight for improvement in how we handle complicated situations in which someone is harmed, so we can finally deliver some long-overdue peace to every single person who has been wronged, hurt, or left feeling silent and alone. We've asked the traumatized millions to quiet down, hold their tongue, and just disappear. So, they go inward, burying their pain to maintain a facade of being "fine." But we all know no one is ever really "fine" after experiences that do so much harm to them emotionally, physically, or psychologically.

How can this be acceptable to us?

I know a fight this big is not just hard, it may seem impossible. What can each of us do to change systems that conspire to shun and minimize people—even unintentionally or unconsciously—who have been abused or traumatized? How can we even start to show up to help? We aren't yet capable of this because we're so used to doing little or nothing to help. Or when we try, we distrust ourselves in the face of something so emotionally messy and hard.

But not trying is not good enough given how many people are suffering around us. Each time we see someone hurting and look the other way, we're compounding their pain. When we pretend it didn't happen, or deny that real, lasting, and life-changing harm was done, we're contributing to their trauma.

This apathy, indifference, and lack of awareness makes recovery much harder and keeps people hidden in darkness. Not because anyone wants to be there alone, but because no one has any idea what to do or how to help. I don't blame people for being unsure of what to do, because the status quo teaches us to look away from so much pain in other people.

Instead of blaming anyone for this huge, sprawling fear of really seeing other people's pain, we can shift our focus to see that our shared fear operates like an unspoken pact and contributes to the silence on this epidemic of pain. It's this silence that makes trauma recovery so difficult for individuals, for organizations, and for our culture that isn't aware of how damaging it is for us.

Think about it like this: what do we tell our kids when they're lost, in trouble, or afraid? We try to reassure them that they will be safe and protected by saying "Ask an adult for help. Tell someone you need them. Tell them what's wrong." We teach them it's courageous to ask for help, and that it shows strength. We ask them to be brave, and to use their voices. We tell them people will hear them if they're able to communicate when something is wrong. We try to reassure them that people will come to their aid. We tell them we're all in this life together, they're not alone, and this is how we take care of each other.

But for so many reasons, this stops working when we're older. In the aftermath of trauma, adults often turn to others for help, but don't get much in return. Most people feel embarrassed and unqualified to offer real help and support and their response is often to freeze. They look away, leaving a victim wondering if they've become invisible. Frozen, their silence often becomes inaction and their failure to act means the trauma continues. And if a victim becomes more vocal in their search for help, other people—the possible helpers—may fear that confronting the problem will spiral out of control. Nearly everyone does what so many other people have done before them out of habit: they bury their heads in the sand, perhaps hoping *it* will go away, but definitely hoping *the victim in pain* will go away, so everyone can move on.

But it doesn't go away. It gets worse for the person who is hurting. The frozen, silent reaction makes understanding trauma doubly hard. This fruitless search for help can feel like being traumatized for a second time.

At this point, many victims start to lose their minds. *How could no one do anything? Why am I dealing with this alone? What the hell is going on here? Can anyone hear me?!* Victims know this feeling: they're struggling to find the right words to communicate their pain, they're using our common language, struggling through their own fear to calmly communicate the facts, and yet . . . nothing happens. Little help comes. Very few people can understand what they're going through. They often remain silent, feeling very alone.

This is the compounded trauma experienced by people around us. Once we realize that we tried to directly address a confusing, terrifying, mental, and physical health-destroying or horrifying experience and nothing changed to protect us, we feel we really are on our own. It is why so many people are living with their silence.

That feeling is among the most caustic realities of being traumatized. That we are fading away into a dark place of terrible isolation where few people can reach us or understand our pain. Our culture of frozen inaction and silence demands that a victim find their *own* way out of a situation that's usually controlled by other people, without any of the support they need. To make it worse, this inaction and fear is subtly telling victims that *they're* somehow at fault for what happened to them. They *asked* for it. They didn't *do* enough to stop it. They *must* have been complicit in some way. They didn't react the right way, they somehow encouraged the abuse, they shouldn't have worn mascara that day, or should have thrown on a sweatshirt, or should have pulled their hair back, maybe should have made less eye contact, stopped smiling, or shouldn't have cracked a joke. It's not that they were in the wrong place at the wrong time. Their existence was the problem.

They should have stopped being themselves altogether, and maybe—just maybe—it wouldn't have happened. We're telling people that the crime of being human, being themselves, and believing they were safe and secure, justifies something traumatic happening in their lives.

But being victimized at any level has nothing to do with what someone was wearing, saying, doing, thinking, how they were behaving, what role they may have been in, where they were, or anything whatsoever within their control. Being victimized is the result of someone else's aggression or violence, or being part of a careless system that didn't protect them. There's no doubt where the fault lies: outside the victim. But that's not how it feels. It feels like being shamed, being blamed, and being forgotten. It feels like being stupid, on top of being in terrible pain, because a victim may have believed they were safe.

We expect victims of trauma to be all-powerful, capable of controlling absolutely everything, including the ability to go back in time to prevent their trauma in the first place. We are asking traumatized people to do impossible things and control everything and everyone in their environment. But that's just not how things work.

Hello, Trauma,

It's been 11 days and I'm still here. I'm lost.

Numbness and sadness are slowly being replaced with fury. I'm dragging myself forward, toward change. I feel bloodied from this emotional crawl.

I'm lost in darkness most of the time, but I'm starting to see glimmers of light. The flicker is small but growing and feels like strength. The more I focus on it, the more I become aware that this is part of the change I need to see, so no one else goes through trauma alone. Silently. I'm not going to take this mutely, slinking away to hide and lick my wounds in darkness. I'm terrified of the darkness. I need to find the light to survive.

I can't tell where this fight is going, but fighting the mess trauma has left me with is my only choice. It's you or me, trauma, and I'm not going to let you win. Damn you, trauma. You are making me really, really mad.

I'm terrified by my feelings, and I need to do something with this fire inside me. I can't sit in darkness, and I won't burn from within. I'm going to fight for myself. No matter what it means, where it takes me, or what it takes from me. I won't stop until what was wrong is made right.

Why is doing the right thing so hard? Why do I have to fight this fight alone? How can I fight when I can't even speak my truth about what happened?

I'm trying to force pain to take a back seat to rage so I can feel more in control of my sadness and confusion. I need to channel my terrible feelings into determination and the outrage that makes this fight a necessity. It's a requirement for my healing. I need to change the depth of my sadness and the sound of my own silence into the kind of deafening noise

I want to see in the world. I want to hear a chorus of people who don't do nothing when they see harm being done, but who will instead stand up for what's right. I had no idea that trauma was so lonely, and I can't live with anyone else feeling this way. Screw you, trauma, I'm going to fight for everyone.

Matt

THREE

Hello Silence

Hello, Trauma,

It's day 37 now, after everything changed.

What are you doing? How could you let this happen? Aren't you better than this? Shouldn't you have known better? How could you be so stupid? What were you doing there anyway?

No one is going to believe you. No one is going to believe that this wasn't all your fault, that you weren't asking for this. They already don't believe you, and you've barely told anyone what happened. They said it was your fault without even saying it. They didn't have to. You know what they mean.

I can feel them blaming me. I can hear them thinking that I'm responsible for this. But how? How did I ask for this horrible experience? Wasn't I just living my life? Since when am I not allowed to do that?

It must be my fault. I should have known better. I should have said something to someone. Maybe I should never have said anything to anyone? What was I wearing that day? I was just being myself. I had no idea this could happen.

Is what happened really assault, though? Am I exaggerating? I'm so confused. Maybe they didn't mean it, and it was just kind of an accident, like, they didn't realize how scared I was? It's probably nothing and I'm making a mountain out of a molehill. Maybe this is just my fear speaking, misfiring, telling me I was in danger, when it was all an innocent mistake or misunderstanding? He would be so embarrassed if this was widely known, and I don't want to ruin his world. It was just a few times. I'm okay. It's fine. I can deal with this. But I'm so confused.

I shouldn't have said anything to anyone. I should have kept my head down. I screwed myself by asking for help. Why aren't I smarter than this? What is wrong with me?

Now I'm dying of shame for two reasons. That this happened in the first place, and that I spoke up. I'm such an idiot. Maybe I had this coming.

Annalise

* * *

Victims of trauma know that speaking up cements their identity as a victim. But remaining silent victimizes them further. The conflicting battle rages in their heads and hearts, and it takes a lot of work to allow the brain to lead. Our brains know right from wrong. Our brains are here to fight to protect us and will not allow abuse to continue or happen to someone else or remain quiet. Our brain knows what the right thing to do is, but our hearts are scared. Terrified, even. Our hearts don't want to be victims, don't want to lose control of ourselves, and don't want to drown in pain. We are afraid of losing it all and living without our stability, privacy, sense of identity, safety, and security.

The reality is, once a person has been victimized, some of this is already lost, through no fault of their own. We sense this but may not see it at first. We know the feeling of control in our lives is slipping through our fingers, but we don't know what to do about it.

One of the biggest challenges facing a victim of trauma is what to do about it. Should they report their abuse? To whom? Should they call the police? Is what's happened to them criminal? Is it just morally wrong? Part of this calculation is how much a victim is willing to detonate the bomb of truth in the environment that allowed their abuse to happen in the first place.

Should they blow up the dysfunction that caused their abuse and trauma to occur, or should they remain silent and accept it? Should they try to quietly address what happened to them and wait for the inevitable fallout as the truth leaks out? Does speaking up and getting no help make their pain worse? Waiting for help makes time feel endless. Remaining silent hurts. Going through the motions destroys the soul and steals all the joy from life. But without a pathway forward, what can be done?

For victims who refuse to allow silence to govern their life—even if *it's been resolved* by other people, those in power—and who refuse to be part of something that allows people to be harmed, deprives them of their voice, and requires them to bury their pain from trauma or abuse, the path is clearer. They choose to fight, choose to speak, and refuse to be silent.

But this means wearing the trauma for all to see. It becomes a scarlet letter for everyone to stare at and speculate about. It brings the potential for so much shame, as consciously and subconsciously, many victims know there is always a group of people who will never believe them. This hurts so much, and there's nothing they can do about it.

When your house is robbed and your television is stolen, you don't have to prove that the TV was there in the first place. Authorities take your word for it, because being robbed means something has been taken from you. But when you're victimized and traumatized by another person, on top of the pain and powerlessness comes the need to prove that it actually happened in the first place. It's even harder to do with a psychological injury.

It takes tremendous courage to say "I will not allow this experience to be swept under the rug. Believe me or don't, but I know what happened because it happened to me." For these victims, the only way forward is to show up authentically, speak the truth, and confront the resistance to their experience, regardless of how awful it can be to fight to be heard. It requires being vulnerable and not accepting silence, even though that means laying bare their worst experiences for others to see, judge, and quantify. But how can we quantify the emotional and psychological injury to another person?

Going through the process of detonating one's security, privacy, and anonymity in pursuit of truth and transparency is like walking through water blindfolded. We may know how to put one foot in front of the other, but it requires our mind and heart to find an autopilot, where their inner voice says "You know what the right thing is, and there's no backing out now. Bring on the blowback." And there is nearly always blowback. The fear that consumes someone as they assert their voice is constant. Every day becomes a deep dive to find the strength to remain committed to what they've started, because there are so many reasons to run and hide, to stop being vulnerable and honest about an awful experience.

Victims fear retaliation from nearly every direction, and for good reason. It can come from the abuser, the organization that didn't react properly or provide sufficient protection, or from literally anyone else out there, as a victim's anonymity and privacy are lost. It's no wonder so many people walk around traumatized and unable to tell anyone. None of us know what more will come our way, making us regret speaking up in the first place.

What a wretched double bind: remain silent and suffer in isolation, and bury your pain, shame, and anxiety. Or speak up, defend yourself, demand justice, refuse to be silenced, and live in fear. It's enough to make a person shut down entirely, going inside and silencing their own voice, which many victims of trauma do. What choice do they have?

* * *

Hello, Trauma,

Day 52

Thinking, spinning, spiraling, floating. I just want these thoughts to stop. Fear, doubt, sadness, what is it that I want . . . calm. I want calm. I want reassurance that I am okay, that I will be okay. That what I am doing is the right thing. The right thing, it always comes back to that. What is the right thing? Speaking up, saying something? Saying something again? When will people hear the words I say? Maybe never the way I want. It took me too long to hear the words I was saying to myself. It still takes me time to make sense of the words in my mind.

I just want these words to stop. Sometimes I just want the world to stop. Maybe I just want someone else to say the words. Not sure what words I want to hear, but I am done hearing nothing. Silence by others is killing me, but I will take my own silence if it can calm my heart.

Listening to the words in my head led me to no longer be silent.

Tracy

* * *

FOUR

Hello Minimization

Hello, Trauma,

It's day 62.

I don't feel well. I'm scared. I'm tired. I'm really upset. I don't know what to do. I can't stand feeling this way and I want to crawl out of my skin.

I'm moving through the motions of getting through the day. I'm tense and anxious, worried about who knows what and what they might say. I'm embarrassed and ashamed as silence falls over any room I walk in. No one will look at me. And when they do, it's like they're looking through me, seeing all my pain and shame. I hate hearing my story through other people. They're wrong about more than they get right. People are just lying, and there's nothing I can do. I don't understand anything.

Someone said I made it all up. I can't imagine why anyone would, but now I'm an attention-seeking liar in some people's eyes. I hate liars.

The rejection and isolation are deadening to me. I'm consumed by the weight of what I've experienced, but I also feel sick that in spite of what it took to say "Enough is enough, I'm not putting up with this abuse for another minute," I don't feel better. Actually, I feel worse, because now I'm so scared. I'm fighting myself, while trying to fight for myself.

The lack of action to protect me is making me feel unstable. Nothing is happening. No one is coming to help. I'm worried about who knows what and what they told others. Why is help taking so long to arrive? Am I being ignored? Is this really happening? I did the right thing, but no one can figure out what the hell they need to do to protect me? This can't be real.

In spite of my fear, I have to keep showing up. What choice do I have? I feel like an inaccurate story has become the narrative of my life, as people tell lies about what happened to me. I can feel the whispers and assumptions. I feel like I'm losing it and I can't trust myself anymore. I am so uncomfortable, I feel shattered.

I can't function in the insanity of knowing that protecting myself was the only choice, while experiencing the most painful loss and consequences for doing the right thing. I wish I could go back in time and react differently, or not react at all. I wish I had a time machine to change this. All of it. No one is taking this seriously, so I'm not even sure I can anymore. Maybe I can just try to forget this happened?

Katherine

* * *

For many victims, minimizing the impact of their trauma comes naturally. No one wants to see themselves as weak, and we tend to be ashamed of having continued feelings about an event that caused us so much pain. We think we should be past it. We struggle to be honest with ourselves because this requires us to face the problem and everything it means. Often, we don't like talking about what happened. We downplay what we survived by telling ourselves it wasn't really a big deal, we should get over it already, and that others have it so much worse. This is our attempt to normalize what's happened to us, as we try to return to a more neutral, approachable, or inviting state to appease others. But this is how we deal with our culture of fear of other people's pain.

We live in a world of toxic positivity. There is a relentless pressure to only display positive emotions and suppress any negative feelings or reactions to the events in our lives. This just invalidates our human experience and reinforces the unhealthiest coping mechanisms, especially for people fighting their way through traumatic experiences.

At its root, we got here by having unrealistic expectations that everything is *all good* (since when?). This forces us to push our sadness and bad feelings down, so we don't appear negative, burdensome, or needy. But goodness, this is yet more hard emotional work. We strive to appear independent, low-maintenance, and in control, but no one anywhere has perfectly happy, conflict-, or challenge-free lives. Trauma makes us *human*, not imperfect or weak. Trauma demands our attention, which is the opposite of being able to let it roll off our backs.

The shame or guilt that comes from being unable to attain the cool, in-control perfection we think others expect of us makes us bury our human nature, which, after a traumatic experience, is being challenged from every direction. This mandate to remain positive, minimizing the negative and damaging things that happen in our lives, is the definition of inauthenticity, though. As hideous as it may be, trauma and the feelings that follow are among our most authentic, honest human experiences.

But the worst part of our social and cultural expectation of relentless positivity is that we're not permitted to fall apart or be human, though sometimes being negative means being honest. It means facing things, rather than thinking "I can't bring my sadness and pain with me. No one can handle it, and it makes me look fragile. Put the mask on." This kind of minimization prevents us from responding appropriately to the many distress signals of trauma—in ourselves or in other people. "It's all good" leads us to offer false, empty reassurances rather than empathy. Without meaning to, we're telling people who are suffering that their feelings have no value. We don't want to hear their truth. We don't want to tell them ours. It's all too hideous to look at, so we don't.

This deepens the negative emotions of a victim or trauma survivor who then may feel guilt for being sad or angry, may hide their painful emotions, and shut down even further. This emotional roller coaster forces trauma to remain trapped. We continue to remain stuck by our unwillingness to face the trauma. We cannot begin to heal in this state due to our emotional limitations on facing pain.

Obviously, life isn't always positive. It denies our emotional truth to force a fake smile, most of the time, because we want to just get along. Sure, having a hopeful outlook is good for our mental health and well-being, but we're not robots. We evolved with a range of emotions for a reason. Some are good and some are there to show us what's wrong, what to avoid, and what we need to fix so we can keep ourselves safe. Trauma is the opposite of safety and there's nothing fake about it. Being positive about it is like lying to ourselves, which takes a lot of work. Doing this for other people as our internal *Enabler* takes over—to get along, to smooth our interactions, and to please other people—is part of why our responses to trauma are hard to correct.

Our negative emotions serve a purpose just as much as our positive feelings do. We can't just cut off or bury the parts and experiences we don't like because they're distasteful to other people or make us seem like we're not fully in control. That's just nonsense. No one is in control all the time, and trauma steals our firm grip on our emotions. Hiding our painful or less appealing feelings destroys trust, vulnerability, authenticity, safety, and security, which are the foundations of our psychological safety in every environment. Hiding these feelings is the opposite of truly caring—about ourselves and our environment.

There's no way to heal from trauma behind the rose-colored glasses of having only positive experiences that discard the truth, minimize and obscure our pain, and force us to cope alone. There is no *looking on the bright side* of being victimized or being traumatized. "Everything happens for a reason" is a lie. People aren't *choosing* to feel the pain of trauma, they have no option. Being faced with a spoken and unspoken requirement to minimize our own painful experiences to appease a cultural mandate that wants us to be perfect leaves us feeling dismissed, ignored, and invalidated.

Most of us already know what being invalidated and dismissed feels like. We don't need the additional shame that comes with having "unacceptable" emotions after trauma and victimization. We can't handle the guilt that is implied in how we're handling our pain wrong, that we're not strong enough to let it roll off our backs, and we don't need more reminders that our authentic human rage and pain are wrong. We can sense that the minimization someone else is showing us is *their* avoidance mechanism. By dodging our complicated feelings, they're sidestepping emotional connections that make *them* feel uncomfortable.

Ignoring these feelings is like muting the pain—the sound is off, but it keeps on playing in the background, subconsciously. Trauma hijacks your reality. It takes over your mind and breaks your heart. It makes you dislike yourself because it makes you feel unworthy. Trauma wants you to be afraid. It wants you to remain vigilant, anxious, hyperalert, freaked out, and upset all the time. But it's not stronger than you are, and it will eventually lose the battle if you engage in the fight for your sanity and mental health.

Trauma wants you to be too scared to look straight at it, or examine it from every angle, or get to the bottom of it. Because once traumatized, your brain sides with your invisible injury to make sure you never get hurt again. The problem is, there may be more trauma down the line, in our own lives, or to our family, friends, or coworkers. Something else might happen that triggers the same fear, anxiety, rage, and powerlessness. So, it's important to negotiate with the hijacker in your mind, to release the hostage: you.

Above all, minimizing the effects of trauma, the complicated, messy, and destructive feelings that follow, prevents our growth. It denies us the need to and ability to confront challenging feelings that allow deeper insight into ourselves and how we heal.

And that's the only point of life after trauma: healing.

* * *

Hello, Trauma,

It's day 77.

I feel invisible. I've never known this feeling before, and it's so strange. I know you are there. I see your reflection every time I walk by the window or mirror. I see you, but you don't look the same. There's a darkness around you now, and the light is gone most days. Where's your light? Are you still there?

I miss seeing myself reflected back. I miss the pep in my step, and the pause in the mirror when I think, damn my hair is on point today. Instead, I see how drained and exhausted I look and feel. Can I keep it together today? What else will someone say about me? But wait. No one is talking about me anymore. It's quiet. I am not relevant anymore. I'm almost forgotten. Erased. I'm invisible.

People are telling me all the ways in which I was wrong, I was crazy, how dare I believe my own experience. Goodness, the things people have said to me and about me. On my best days, I laugh at the insanity that people have the audacity to say these things to a victim, oh there's that word again, but the reality is their words do make me feel crazy and question the meaning of my actions. They make me doubt everything about myself.

Damn, the amount of questioning, minimizing, then abusing me for just standing up for what's right is disgusting. I'm still here, but no one knows, because I'm silent in this trauma.

Sue

* * *

FIVE

Hello Gaslighting

Hello, Trauma,

It's day 99.

The only power I have now is to show up looking and acting "okay," yet there's nowhere for me to put these feelings, which eat away at me. I don't want to be viewed as weak. I am working day and night to heal this wound, but what I can't talk about blocks literally everything else, including the joy, the light, and the peace in my life.

My disappearance only leads to the projections in other people, like they're painting the canvas of my life and I have no way of stopping them. Where did I go? Can I ever find my way back? I can't tell what's real and what's my emotional mess anymore. I don't know what to believe. Or who to trust. Or who to believe and count on. None of this makes any sense to me.

Lucie

* * *

This is where gaslighting and its effects enter the aftermath of trauma, making victims doubt their sanity and challenging their truth. After trauma, the pain of trying to convince everyone of the facts of the experience leaves sufferers questioning their own version of events. This creates constant self-doubt, confusion, heightened anxiety, and depression. Gaslighting makes us question our own reality. Low self-esteem, disorientation, and being silenced contribute to post traumatic stress, as victims begin to doubt their own perceptions, feelings, and memory, which bleeds into every part of their lives. Overall, gaslighting makes people feel like they've lost all control over their lives as they lose trust in their own judgment and reality.

The root of gaslighting is a desire to gain power over others. As victims of trauma already know, the powerlessness created by their experience and feelings are already making them feel foggy and confused. That's exactly the point. A person on the receiving end of this kind of manipulation is already struggling with the deepest confusion as they try to understand what's happening to their mind, body, and recollection of events.

Victims of trauma may not know that they're being gaslit—either by their abuser, by those they try to seek help from, or by our culture that doesn't acknowledge how common trauma is—but the experience is consistent and predictable. It leads to censoring an already confused, reactive, and upset victim. To be clear: not all gaslighting is on purpose. It's an outcome of our discomfort with really looking at trauma and its victims in the face. But it's as common as trauma itself, since we aren't skilled at empathetically helping to heal the damage of so much trauma in our environment.

Some of the common tactics used to gaslight and silence victims are **countering**, in which an abusive person or organization questions someone's memory of events, even when a victim is clearly communicating their memory of the truth. There is also **withholding**, when someone pretends not to understand something, or refuses to listen. **Trivializing** occurs when an abusive person or environment makes a victim's feelings, concerns, or fear seem unimportant or irrational, overblown, and hysterical. **Diverting and blocking** is when an abusive person changes the subject or focuses on the credibility of what someone is saying rather than the content itself.

All of this may be happening consciously or subconsciously, but the effect is the same: that a victim feels out of control and out of their mind. That's the point. It makes the problem and the victim go silent, go away, and take their trauma and victimization with them. Gaslighting is not just limited to intimate relationships. It can happen in professional and social environments too. Like when an organization portrays someone who has the courage to speak up against abuse as irrational, crazy, deluded, hypersensitive, or attention-seeking. This makes getting help so much harder. It also makes pushing for change virtually impossible, as though one person is trying to stop a flash flood alone.

The result silences victims of trauma. That's what the subtle manipulation of gaslighting is intended to do. And it doesn't only impact *one* victim, but also anyone else who may experience something their environment is telling them to remain quiet about. It's like the environment whispers: "We won't listen, so you might as well remain silent."

It can take years to recover one's self-esteem and heal from the deadening, silencing effect of gaslighting. For many victims, the kind of work it requires feels impossible. How can a victim even start to heal when he or she can't be heard or understood? It begins with accepting that we aren't responsible for someone else's abusive behavior or others' inadequate reactions. We must place blame *outside* ourselves so we can practice listening to our own thoughts, feelings, instincts, and memories again.

This is incredibly difficult to do in the beginning. There are so many other voices competing for a trauma victim's attention, voices screaming that it wasn't that bad, that it's in the past, that they're okay, that they should be over the bad feelings by now, that the bad dreams, anxiety, depression, or sadness are about something else, that they're weak, fragile, or "damaged," and that their trauma doesn't matter. But of course, it *does* matter. It left an invisible scar that can't heal as others deny the trauma. A victim themself may deny it, too, because it's painful to examine and too hard to do alone. Making sense of the confusion after trauma and the gaslighting that often follows takes a lot of time, time a victim feels they don't have, because this is hard work.

But feeling our way through this deep tunnel of confusion is important. If we don't, we can never get back to a place where we can hear and trust our own voice again. Where we can believe what our senses are telling us, and where we can have complete faith in our ability to keep ourselves safe. We can't rely on ourselves without these things. We can't be mindful of our own emotions, and we will be forced to abandon our own intuition. Gaslighting and the aftermath of trauma try to silence not only our reality, but our well-honed internal security system: our gut that whispers to our brains that something is off, wrong, or dangerous, which puts us in danger every time we ignore that inner voice.

Gaslighting also works to negate our personal values. It tries to tell us that what we know to be right and wrong is off balance, incorrect, or not the truth. This kind of manipulation demands that we abandon our standards, handing more control to either an abuser, the system that abused us, or the painful aftermath of abuse, to gain more control over us. But without our highest values, we are actually in constant danger, because we'll accept behaviors and mistreatment that harm us further.

It's also common to gaslight ourselves after trauma. We do this by thinking we've overreacted. Chances are, we didn't. When we start to leave a state of shock, we can become ashamed of how emotional we were, what we said or did, and how hard or loudly we reacted to protect ourselves. Our first reaction is usually the most honest. We need to forgive ourselves for our normal, healthy reaction to any kind of fear, fight, flight, freezing, or fawning.

At a moment when a victim of trauma is already scared, anxious, struggling to trust themselves in order to protect themselves, questioning their memory, judgment, and voice, this added level of confusion can be devastating. That's why it's so important to take some time to think deeply. To really listen to that quiet, injured inner voice that's trying to be heard. Until we can really listen, we can't hear ourselves. And if we can't hear ourselves, we can't start to heal.

* * *

Hello, Trauma,

It's day 512.

I see you pretty clearly now. It's sunny out. But I see you. I see me. I sit here feeling the sun. As I reflect on where I've been, who I was, who I've become, I finally see you. I feel you. I see the world. It's different and changed. But I'm here.

You know, I once thought that I was completely broken. Well, I didn't want to admit I was broken, if I'm being real. Maybe cracked . . . when bad things happen, when the words that I had a hard time saying and were hard to admit . . . when trauma occurred. I had to decode what trauma was.

What was traumatic? What did I experience that was traumatic? I had to own that I was a victim. Owning that allowed me to feel broken. But I just wanted to be cracked, not fully broken. I wanted to be whole, but I couldn't. I couldn't deny what I was, or what had happened. Something did happen, there's no denying that.

And I wanted to just be a little bit broken, not fully. Still together, still whole. But the cracks were getting bigger. The denial of the trauma was growing, the denial of the emotions was eating me alive, and the denial of the pain was breaking me.

And it wasn't until I truly allowed myself to crumble that I think I began to heal. I don't know if we ever really allow ourselves to crumble when we're such strong- headed people. We don't want to admit weakness or whatever prevents us from actually being sad, anxious, depressed, worried, alone with people in pain, or whatever it was that stopped me. But refusing to admit my reality and confront my pain held me back.

When I actually admitted I wasn't okay, I crumbled, I broke, and I could breathe. But allowing myself the cathartic release of crying and raging and spiraling and sitting, I became different. Anyone would become different and would have to change from this.

The way you see the world is different when things happen, when trauma occurs, when you identify as a victim—the world changes. I changed. But I didn't like the darkness and didn't want to be there. I don't want the darkness to come in again.

But it will. It does. It has. But today it's sunny. Today the world is different. You know, a part of becoming whole again is becoming different and really accepting that I've changed. But I'm still me. Or maybe I'm me again. And maybe the cracks are put back together, and the scars healed a little bit differently.

What I once knew is different from what I know now, how I experience, how I show up, how I flinch at the sign of things, how I will break down in tears when I truly spend time thinking about what happened as the anger surfaces so quickly.

But when the sun's out, when I sit and I feel who I want to be, I am okay. The colors are back. I'm vibrant again. I can live and I can be free. But it truly is the breaking of who I once was that allows me to become who I am now and how I show up and how I see things.

The clouds will come again. And maybe that's the reflection I have now. I can be and I can see the world, but I can see myself and I can be who I want to be and take control over that. I am strong. I feel a little better—safer and more in control. I'm no longer broken, and the relief is like nothing I've ever felt before.

Hailey

SIX

Hello Shame

Hello, Trauma,

It's day 2. I'm inconsolable.

Anger. Rage. Embarrassment. Wipe your tears away. Hold your head high. You. Did. Nothing. Wrong. Breathe. Breathe. Breathe. My anger is hard to control. I feel I am losing my mind. I'm going crazy, and how can no one see how totally and completely wrong this is?

I walked away alone. I walked away as a shell, forced to suffer in silence, in public, and without the acknowledgment that's caused me to move through the world in silence. There is no acknowledgment of what was happening, just the pure isolation of a place that isn't safe. For me, for anyone else, and for everyone in their orbit. How can I be the only one who feels so much shame? Where is their shame? Why aren't they falling all over themselves to apologize to me? I'm the one traumatized, and they just keep going, like it never happened. In trauma, rarely is there any finality of "resolution," because it's not resolved for me, only for them. So I'm the one left with isolation and shame? Why?

Kayla

* * *

As victims of trauma work to heal, it's normal to feel like an exposed nerve of pain, with none of the trust that enables them to feel safe. Trust is the foundation of psychological safety and security. These terms are used a lot but are often misunderstood by people and organizations.

Simply put, why psychological safety and security exist, there is a sense of trust and permission to be candid, honest, and vulnerable. They mean we can create space for people to be secure, not just safe. They also mean there will be no retribution for being open and speaking up, voicing an opinion or a concern. Environments that encourage, recognize, and reward people for taking the risk of speaking up—especially when something damaging and destructive is going on—don't leave people feeling broken, weak, or traumatized. In essence, psychologically secure environments create conditions where safety is possible for everyone.

Think about it this way: when we get in a car, a warning reminds us to put our seatbelt on. The seatbelt creates security so we can remain as safe as possible. The seatbelt isn't guaranteed to protect us from injury, but it can reduce the harm if something goes wrong. Knowing it's there makes us feel safe, and that we've put all necessary measures in place that are within our control. Security is something else, though. It assists and supports safety—it's the emergency services that arrive if we need them—because we can't guarantee safety from all outside variables. But we can use the tools that make us as secure as possible every time we get in a car.

People can be themselves when they feel safe, and they can form the kinds of bonds and connections that protect themselves and others. Their questions get answered. Their concerns are taken seriously. Their requests for help and support lead to action. Their humanity, contribution, and well-being are prioritized. Their fear is everyone's concern.

What psychological safety and security isn't, within a team or organization, is a shield from accountability, coddling, insincere niceness, political correctness, or infantilization. It's not looking the other way when someone doesn't perform or fulfill their responsibilities, or leaves the people around them hanging, burdened by pulling the weight of someone who is disengaged. It's not a kind of diplomatic immunity to behave any way we want, refusing to adhere to basic rules of conduct and behavior and insisting that our boundaries have been violated, so we evade responsibility. And it doesn't mean always being "nice" because people are too sensitive. Being collegial to a fault only creates insincere and false harmony. That's inauthentic and dishonest and the opposite of real safety and security.

Here's why psychological safety and security are so important in our environments: they affect our physical and mental health. When we experience these things, we feel more confident and freer. More importantly, we feel less anxiety, fear, and depression. We're more engaged, inclusive, collaborative, creative, kind, and compassionate. We care more about fostering an environment where people want to be, and want to stay, because they feel valued and prioritized. Our teams are stronger, our relationships are more durable, and we can be our best selves.

This is as important in our work and social lives as it is in our intimate relationships, and the benefits are enormous. When people feel safe and secure at work, it's easier for them to be present and more engaged. Their creativity is supported and new ideas flourish because people feel allowed to express themselves. We feel encouraged to take more risks. We communicate better, resolve conflict more fairly, show more empathy, are more vulnerable, and listen more actively.

All of this promotes and leads to more respect because it supports connecting and belonging. In this environment, we know that we will be accepted for who we are. We can't be ourselves where we don't feel safe. We can't be healthy where we feel insecure. And we can't heal or process trauma where none of this is possible. Nor can we prevent trauma from happening in the first place. An absence of psychological safety and security also shames people for natural and human responses to feeling unsafe or insecure. This keeps our collective trauma alive and prevents healing.

Shame is a very strange thing. It's not guilt, which is a sense that "I did something wrong." Shame feels like "I am bad. I am not worth better than this. I am at fault for what's wrong here." It makes us feel like everyone can see into us and they dislike what they see. If guilt focuses on behavior, shame is an assessment of our character traits. When people experience shame, they feel worthless, exposed, afraid to look stupid, but they're *convinced* they already do. It leads us to worry constantly about what other people think about us, while disliking and judging ourselves. It can lead to an anxious sense of seeking perfection so we don't fail and expose ourselves to yet *more* shame, and it creates relentless negative self-talk.

People trying to recover from trauma are trapped in the deepest, darkest shame, and their inner voice becomes their worst critic. They don't want to change their character, because chances are, they like who they are, or did, before their traumatic experience. They respect themselves, or used to before they were victimized. They may not have been ashamed of themselves before their trauma, and they may have had a more stable, secure, and kinder understanding of who they are, where they fit in the world, and how they showed up in their lives. But being victimized can cause toxic shame, an intense feeling of self-loathing and judgment that keeps coming up.

As shame becomes more frequent or intense—especially in the dark aftermath of traumatic experiences—it makes a person question their worth. They feel not good enough, weak, unable to protect themselves, useless, valueless, invisible, and disposable. People with toxic shame internalize the message that being victimized was *their* fault, they didn't deserve better, and being silenced as they sought help and support is *also* their fault, not the failure of psychologically unsafe places and systems that are failing to protect them.

Unlike ordinary shame or feeling foolish—which we've all felt from time to time—toxic shame creates a feeling of chronic, grinding worthlessness in some trauma victims. This intense, overpowering, and crushing shame floods back any time a person is triggered. It makes people lose compassion for themselves and unable to show themselves empathy. It can lead us to withdraw from others and become defensive, distant, and silent, as we lose the ability to connect and communicate how we really feel. Shame makes people feel like their human emotions aren't important and no one would care anyway, so burying feelings and going quiet seems like the only way to live. Self-destructive behavior follows, because shame causes people to feel as though they're flawed at their core and not worthy of better treatment. In return they treat themselves badly.

Physiologically, the brain reacts as if it were facing physical danger, activating the fight, flight, freeze, or fawn response. The flight response triggers the feeling of needing to disappear; trauma victims experience deep shame and believe they have become invisible. They feel powerless. The fight response makes ashamed people extremely reactive. The freeze response emotionally paralyzes us, and fawning leads us to empathize with our abusers instead of ourselves. All of this upsets our ability to think clearly. We're left feeling like there is something wrong with *us* because we *deserve* this. Clearly, being victimized and traumatized is never our fault. But our brains don't know this.

Here's why: since birth, our brains have been hard at work storing information in our amygdala, the core of a neural system built for processing fearful or threatening stimulation, about how our needs were or were not met by our caregivers. The amygdala is part of the limbic system within the brain, which helps us process emotions, survival instincts, and memory. It works unconsciously to regulate our behavior and physiological responses. When we feel stressed or afraid, it releases stress hormones that prepare the body to fight the threat or flee the danger. But so many common, everyday emotions trigger this response, like fear, anger, anxiety, and aggression. Being a survivor of trauma co-opts this hypersensitive system and makes nearly everything a trigger.

The silence it imposes becomes a trigger. Feeling powerless triggers us. The fear of our memories triggers us. We are left in a constantly reactive state and always on edge.

Shame can lead to more shame—a paradoxical spiral in which feeling shame leads to being ashamed of feeling shame. Trauma victims know this all too well. These confusing feelings show up every day and come from both internal and external directions. What we tell ourselves—that we deserved it—and what others telegraph to us—that they're uncomfortable with what happened to us—make us feel out of our minds. It seems as though they are *also* ashamed of us. The messages come from so many directions that we often have no idea what's *our* shame and what's *theirs*.

This sensitive shame-signaling doesn't even need to be spoken out loud to be heard crystal clear by someone lost in the darkness of trauma. "You should have known better," "What did you expect," or "Why didn't you do more to stop it?" attacks our humanity and straddles both the overt and covert information our amygdala are working hard to process. But, as shame mandates, we can't scream that we have *done nothing wrong, we* are the victim, *we* need help, not more judgment. In these moments, we no longer feel like a person. Instead, our trauma is compounded by a toxic culture, the absence of psychological safety and security, and the little compassion we find leaves us helpless.

Humans need to belong, in our relationships, our social groups, our workplaces, and our communities. Rejection and exclusion hurt us deeply and feel like a social death penalty, especially when we have the courage to ask for help but don't get it. This makes us feel shunned and ostracized, which further attacks our low self-esteem.

Being frozen out is among the most devastating experiences we can endure regardless if it's on the playground or workplace, since it's so deeply connected to our most fundamental need to be accepted and recognized by others. Ostracization is a controlling form of behavior that expresses a group's fear. It's an attempt to neutralize a threat by punishing someone who challenges a system or group, and creates "insiders" and "outsiders."

For the person being shunned, the effects are devastating. Feelings of being on the outside have been known to create extreme anxiety, depression, self-hatred, increased blood pressure, loss of appetite, self-injury, suicidal thoughts or attempts, and rage that can veer into violence. Being shunned after trauma is several steps too far for our sensitive systems, which just want to be included, protected, and safe.

When we are excluded, our brains release an enzyme that attacks the hippocampus, which is responsible for regulating how our neurons connect and communicate throughout our nervous systems. This throws us into fight, flight, freeze, or fawn mode, as our brain focuses only on what it must do to survive. Instead of being comfortable as part of the tribe, our brains are constantly scanning our environments and our interactions to determine if we "fit in" or are at risk of being cast out, alone.

As we experience these intense surges of hormones, our brains shrink our available memory, so we're not distracted by other ideas, information, or stray thoughts. This makes it much harder for us to solve problems effectively. We become more reactive, as the amygdala goes into overdrive and reduces our self-control. For victims of trauma, who are already suffering and seeking connection and support from their "tribe," resignation can feel like the only option. Giving up, falling silent, and disappearing to protect themselves makes sense, as they feel they've already lost all control. This can create even more confusion and doubt about who they are, where they belong, and who they can trust.

Is it *really* possible that no one has our backs? Are we *really* so low value? Are we *really* entirely alone? Is no one *really* listening or willing to help? Are we *really* in this fight with silence and pain alone? Is everything else—reputation, money, the status quo, keeping up the appearance of being "okay," keeping the peace—so much more important than the victims themselves? This is the psychological danger of being traumatized. We are filled with shame, unable to process it, and unable to get the help and support we need, while being shunned in the pursuit of help.

This fact, for so many victims, is particularly hard to swallow. In the aftermath of trauma, feeling our value slip through our fingers shakes us to the core as we realize that all those relationships we counted on, that were built on trust and vulnerability, may have been transactional or just going along to get along. We lose compassion for ourselves and others, as the pain of trauma deepens. Trauma tests our patience in ways that deepen anxiety, and when you're struggling in trauma's aftermath, patience is the last thing you have.

* * *

Hello, Trauma,

It's day 22.

It's hot and I ran, for miles and miles, forcing one more step, then another, then miles more. It was as though I was trying to run from the problem, but we know how that works. Though I was moving, I was going nowhere. Running releases my anger, frees my mind, and blunts the sharp edges of too much thinking, but I'm still left with the dull, empty sadness of my fear, anger, and pain, and I feel like a permanent outsider now.

I have no patience for this. So I shopped. Retail therapy didn't help, so I sat and wrote. I tried to make sense of my thoughts, since sense and meaning are my superpowers, but nothing changed. I cried. Anywhere, at any moment, the tears came and didn't stop.

I cranked the music, since it connects to my heart like nothing else can. It calmed my mind for a moment, stopped the screaming between my ears, and I felt a smile—the first in a while. For a moment, I remembered who I was before everything happened, and felt a momentary sense I may have turned a corner. Perhaps I was out of the woods?

Of course, I wasn't. I was just on one of the plateaus of making sense of trauma, in which I briefly gained access to myself. Is this the way it's always going to be now? I'm afraid of everything and everyone. I'm stuck in a process that excludes my voice, since I have to be silent about what happened to me, while I wait—patiently—for some resolution.

I don't "trust in this process." I don't believe that the right thing will happen. I don't trust or believe anyone right now, and my shame and anger are making me sick. This waiting is worse than anything I've ever been through, as I wonder if anything will actually happen to fix this.

They tell me "it will be resolved," but does that mean fairly? Does that mean anyone will hear and believe me? Waiting in the wake of this trauma is hell and I can't hold my breath much longer. I'm in a nightmare I can't wake up from, and I have no control over my own story. Is my life even my own at this point? It doesn't feel that way.

Ashley

SEVEN

Hello Fear

Hello, Fear,

It's day 82.

The fear is coming from everywhere. Will I let others down if I admit the truth about what's happening? Will I be blamed for someone else's actions?

Once I finally admitted the truth to myself, I had to accept and embrace what being a victim means. We all understand the word, but I had to absorb it into myself. Being a victim means pain.

Wasn't I supposed to be able to take it and just move on? I can't. I shouldn't have to. No one should. Fighting the truth in myself, I'm getting worse, not better.

I was acting as all others did in a state of trauma, and I shamed myself. I should have been able to stop this from happening. But how? I even feel this way now: I should know better. I am not powerless. I can only be powerless if I give my power to others. If I allow others to make me feel less than, make me feel the blame. But here's the thing: I know the words. But the words aren't feelings, they're just how we transact with each other.

Intellectually, I know I wasn't powerless, but instead: I'm able to right a wrong, strong enough to speak truth to power, and solve problems. I know who I am. I value myself as much as I value other people. But this is the conflict so many trauma victims vacillate between.

But I'm so scared.

Kris

* * *

One of the many painful and confusing issues that being a victim brings up for trauma survivors is watching other people take control of the narrative of our experience without our consent or input. This silencing happens when others diminish, ignore, minimize, or override who we are and assume control of our story. It makes it hard for victims to tell our *own* stories, and because shame is already in the driver's seat, it just silences trauma survivors even further. Many women know this feeling deep in our souls. We know how hard it is to speak up in the first place, and it's especially hard when others decide to do the talking for us.

But why?

Both men and women struggle to report being victims of abuse or violence, but with different psychological landscapes. Women are so routinely discredited, discounted, gaslit, minimized, or deleted from their own stories that they often don't believe *each other* or *themselves*. Our fear of shaming, blaming, of being accused of exaggerating or seeking attention, and our terror of retaliation, ostracization, or that we "misunderstood" being victimized makes controlling our own stories virtually impossible.

The statistics reveal this truth. According to the National Sexual Violence Resource Center, one in five women and one in sixteen men are sexually assaulted while in college, though more than 90 percent of sexual assault victims of either gender on college campuses never report their assault. Rape is the most under-reported crime: 63 percent of sexual assaults aren't reported to the police; nearly one in ten women have been raped by an intimate partner in her lifetime; and 82 percent of all juvenile sexual assault victims are female. According to the Rape, Abuse & Incest National Network, every sixty-eight seconds an American is sexually assaulted, and every nine minutes that victim is a child, usually a girl. According to the United Nations, 49 percent of women experiencing domestic violence never report their cases or seek help.

These statistics may shock you. Maybe not. Or they may be too much to really take in. But these numbers represent *people*, and they have meaning. They carry tremendous weight for every person who becomes part of them. Those of us brave enough to look closer at the numbers help tell the story so many people are afraid to talk about. The point of highlighting these statistics is to show that for both male and female survivors of assault, abuse, and sexual violence, reporting their trauma is so hard that many believe there will be no benefit to them. Instead, they go silent. Many survivors don't think they'll be taken seriously by authorities, don't know who to tell, or are too afraid to speak out.

They sense on a subconscious level that instead of their testimony or experiences being considered valid, they will not be granted the benefit of the doubt. Some anticipate being called a liar. They know they will pay a price for going public about what happened to them. They will be asked to prove the often unprovable, recount the horrific details of what has happened to them, and call themselves a victim publicly. They know that we live in a culture that doesn't always deliver the consequences of aggression onto *aggressors*, but instead, asks victims to get out of the way of aggression, rather than forcing it to stop. They expect to be trivialized, and sense that speaking out will take over their whole lives, and they may not want to lose even more of themselves.

Studies show that men and women deal with trauma differently and that PTSD is more common in women than in men. According to the National Center for PTSD, around 10 percent of women will have PTSD at some point in their lives compared to 4 percent of men. This makes women twice as likely to develop the scary, intrusive memories, avoidance coping mechanisms, and changes in thinking, mood, and behavior that follow a traumatic experience. Considering that about 60 percent of men and 50 percent of women experience at least one traumatic event in their lifetime, this is a very large group of people.

The differences in how men and women process their traumatic experiences may account in part for why so many more women develop PTSD than men. The types of traumas each gender experiences are another significant factor. Women are more likely to be victims of rape, sexual assault, and sexual abuse as a child, which all have a higher risk of PTSD. Men, on the other hand, while still vulnerable to sexual abuse, are more likely to encounter traumas like physical assault, combat, and accidents of all kinds. The effects of sexual assault are destructive to any victim, but especially for women: 94 percent of adult female victims experience PTSD within the first two weeks following their attack.

Another reason women are at increased risk of PTSD is that in communities where more traditional gender roles are the norm—in which men have more power than women—women tend to feel more emotionally vulnerable. In this type of environment, women lean into more of a "tend and befriend" coping strategy.

Tending involves taking care of the people around us, while befriending is the process of trying to connect with others to find relief from distress and pain. Considering that women are often more emotionally reliant on their social networks than men—borne of more talking and connecting over emotional issues—women are more likely to experience PTSD symptoms if their social network is unsupportive in their time of need, or if they feel rejected, abandoned, and shunned.

Our society teaches men that anger is a sign of strength and power, even when it's a response to fear, anxiety, depression, or sadness. Trauma is a particularly difficult subject for men to talk about, since we expect them to be tough, strong, and able to protect themselves, and not show emotional vulnerability. These expectations can cause men to ignore, minimize, and bury the trauma in their lives at even higher levels than women, who have more freedom to show an emotional range.

We discourage boys from showing their emotions. Instead, we teach them that strength, confidence, success, and mastery of everything they do are the characteristics we value most in them, and that showing any distress means they're being weak or feminine. It's hard for anyone to accept the role of "victim," but it's particularly difficult for men. There is an unspoken expectation that they be in control of themselves, more than what we expect of women. This is the impact of systemic trauma: for all victims of trauma, of all genders, we know that speaking their truth will bring a new wave of a personalized traumatic experience to overcome due to the features of our environment that give rise to trauma, maintain it, and impact our post-traumatic responses.

* * *

Being unable to tell your own story is like the nightmare of opening your mouth to speak and finding no sound, just barren silence. It's an emptiness where your voice should be, with dozens of conflicting thoughts burying you. Speaking out publicly about what's happened invites anonymous strangers to attack victims, sexualize them, and turn their anger on already traumatized people, while releasing their frustration about the systemic trauma *they've* experienced because a victim dared to react publicly to what happened. Victims are damned if they do speak up and damned if they don't. Being alone in trauma is difficult, but revealing it puts them at risk for the worst invalidation.

After the fact, many victims are forced to confront a new reality they could not see coming: the suggestion that they lied. That they made it all up. That they have grim, active imaginations, and they created a story of trauma in their lives, for god knows what reason. No one would choose to make this up. Why on earth would anyone imagine that a victim of abuse or trauma has invented a story, a story in which only *they* lose? Why would anyone enlist to be the subject of endless conjecture and assumption, earning themself infamy in the process?

Why would anyone make up the worst event in their life in order to constantly be forced to defend their actions, choices, what they wore, where they went, how they respond to anything and everything, what they say, and how the processing of their trauma is perceived by others? They wouldn't, is the answer. No true victim of trauma would intentionally choose to lie about events that have caused them so much pain. Sure, there have been rare instances of malicious, selfish, or unstable people who made up false accusations. But the overwhelming majority of people would never choose to feel this low, this drained, this sad, angry, lonely, empty, abandoned, and cast out.

What we should be asking is, why are so many people traumatized? Why is it so hard to talk about it? Why is the truth so hard for us to accept? Why don't we focus on the reality that trauma *does* happen to so many people and we're badly prepared to deal with it? Since an estimated 70 percent of adults in the United States have experienced some kind of traumatic event at least once in their lives, that means over 223 million people have some personal experience with trauma, according to the National Council for Behavioral Health. That's *more* people with trauma in their minds and bodies than those who *haven't* experienced trauma.

* * *

Hello, Trauma,

Day 39 here.

My life has shifted to protecting myself and my family, always having to be conscious of where I am, who knows I'm there, who might come up behind me. I get flashes of panic as I imagine living my old life. Should I go to the dog park, where people know me and know what happened to me? Should I compete in that triathlon I was training for before all this happened? If I do, what risks of further anxiety, fear, and panic am I exposing myself to because people know? Can I go on that interview, knowing they may have heard about me?

What about just living a small life? Is the supermarket safe? What about a restaurant? Am I safe just walking alone as I used to do?

Now I protect myself everywhere. At all times, even in private, I'm on guard about how I communicate, post anything online, and show up in any space I need or want to be in. I had to change and live in constant awareness of what I'm doing, everywhere, all day and night, but no one else did. Not the system that allowed me to become traumatized or the people who operate in the system, because for them, I was erased.

Natalie

* * *

EIGHT

Hello Truth

Hello, Truth,

It's been 210 days.

My dad always taught me to be the bigger person, to show up, to do the right thing. Rules are rules and deals are deals, but damn, my brain is twisted with this event in my life. What is the right thing when you experience such wrong? Is my version of "right" the same as yours? I mean, we all grew up differently, we all see the world differently, but where some issues are concerned, isn't there always a "right thing"?

I thought there was, but as I experience this, as I watch my friends go through things, the right thing is never happening, and the right thing is always different than what you saw in your mind. "The right thing." What does that even mean? To do no wrong? To help people when they have been hurt? To show up or stop something wrong from happening? To make sure people are safe? To be a good human? Just be a good person, no matter what else is happening or whatever anyone else is doing. Doing the right thing is so hard for people, and I'm so confused as to why.

Maybe I'm wrong for judging and assuming I know what the right thing is. I watch when people don't do the right thing when I think they should. We all just take out our phones and record hideous things, but don't step in. We send quiet, supportive messages to victims, but we don't speak out publicly. Why? Is there too much risk, even for bystanders?

Doing the right thing is using your voice, your power, your place in the world to step up and make others feel safe, to function in common care and humanity for others. It's hard because we all see the world differently. But also, because we're selfish.

We protect ourselves first and we fear stepping out of our lanes to protect other people. We worry that doing the right thing may impact us or threaten us somehow, so we don't do anything. Is this selfish or just self-protective?

I guess I understand when others didn't step in or didn't help me or helped only when the risk to someone else passed. But what I wish the most was that you wanted to help, even when it was hard or risky. I wish that your anger was as big as mine and that you felt my pain and you felt this shouldn't have happened. I wish that you shared my view that we should hold people accountable, even if we don't have control of the outcome. I wish you had still shown up and stood up for the right thing with me. It would have changed everything for me.

Tyler

* * *

I believe in the good in humanity, that most people were raised to do the right thing. But systemic trauma and so few psychologically safe and secure places leave many of us unsure of what we can do to help, how we can stand up for what's right, and how to defend ourselves and others.

This is true for both men and women, though people get particularly confused when a woman defends herself and demands psychological safety and security, especially after a traumatic experience. Many women feel guilty for setting boundaries, specifically in the workplace. Often raised to be more people-pleasing than men, women experience anxiety when putting their own needs and concerns first. They fear conflict, rejection, and judgment when they assert their need for safety and security rather than compromise their feelings.

The evidence of this is everywhere. For women trying to work through trauma, the big-picture details tell the story of environments where trauma is tolerated and the lack of psychological safety and security that results. Women are still paid about 82 percent of a man's salary for the same work, still make up a majority of support or care-taking jobs, are still harassed, are more fearful of violent crime than men are, and still live in a culture where images of women being victimized and attacked are so common that we barely notice how much abuse has been laundered into our mainstream consciousness.

Even just reacting to this constant, unsubtle message of "be afraid, all the time" is met with resistance, as though we're being hypersensitive. Acknowledging how unsafe and insecure many environments are feels like taking a personal risk, and leaves women vulnerable to being perceived as acting like a victim, "difficult" or over-reactive.

Here's the thing: women are trained to *under*react, not the opposite. We're socialized to minimize our experiences, both good and bad. We're supposed to take nearly whatever comes our way and accept the judgment from men and other women. We're taught to gaslight ourselves before anyone else has the chance to do it because even the act of standing up for ourselves often leads to "Who does she think *she* is?" and "Oh, come on, it wasn't *that* bad." And even if we do find the courage to speak up, we're met with the clear message that we're not being taken seriously. Girls learn early that their boundaries may not fit in the world, so women become skilled at making theirs flexible, to accommodate other people even though we may not feel entirely safe.

Every woman reading this probably knows this fog and how isolating it is. Every woman knows how it's possible to become paranoid alone in the fog. And why wouldn't we get scared and minimize our own fear or concerns? It's not clear if anyone is listening. They *can't* listen if women can't speak, and a lot of the time most women feel they can't. They can't because, all too often, they're silenced by a culture that minimizes traumatic experiences. And they're silent because of how bad it can feel after trauma has happened in their life.

This silence is the first thing we can change about how we understand and heal from trauma.

What does it mean to be silenced? Or to be silent? They're two very different things. Most victims of trauma don't choose to be silent. But in very meaningful ways, they are because they have to be. Sometimes silence as a response to trauma is the only thing that makes sense. A person needs to stop communicating to process an experience. Others use silence as a way to punish. For many people, falling silent is a way to control our anger, which would make a bad situation worse, but anger is a natural, normal response. It takes a great deal of control and focus to do something that isn't the right thing to do in the first place—silencing ourselves.

This silence mocks us, as though we're invisible. Nothing stops anyone from letting a victim know what they really think, harassing them, and keeping them looking over their shoulders at all times. It only stops *the victim's* ability to respond. It stops our ability to assert an honest defense, tell the truth, and scream "This is wrong. This should never have happened. Where is the empathy?"

* * *

Hello, Trauma,

It's day 52.

This forced silence feels like a massive gash, left open and prone to infection. Plenty of random dirt gets into this wound, as other voices add their interpretations to the chorus. This silence breaks my heart, it hurts my head, and it changes my emotional structure. I feel as though I have lost not only my voice, but also my identity. Isn't that what being forced into silence does? It takes away a big part of who we are.

It gnaws at me, grinding my feelings, and hits me like a truck each time I see that someone has written, spoken, or rendered a verdict on me, my life, and my experience without my input. But I can't scream in this jagged silence.

There are times when I feel like I'm drowning. I'm at the bottom of the pool, the water pressure is pushing on my lungs, and holding my breath is getting harder with each second. I'm drowning in my thoughts, drowning in silence. Hearing the world speak about me, reading the words written about me, and feeling every single lie like a red-hot cattle brand on my skin. The abuse, harassment, threats, the questions I can't answer—they're all like drowning in clean air, bright sunlight, and total dryness. The air has become deep water. My thoughts feel deadly, and a part of me has died, because she couldn't breathe, couldn't speak, and she became a disembodied witness to her own story.

This loss of control and the surreal identity shift that's come with it have redrawn the boundaries of who I am. I could accept this if it had come with some accountability, but it didn't. The story stops when you're silenced. All that's left is for other people to tell your story in any way that fits their narrative.

There was no other way. This was the only solution available to me. It all happened so fast, once something happened, and I barely had time to think. I had been alone in the silence for so long at that point. I would have given virtually anything to be free for a moment. So, I surrendered to the silence and agreed to be silent. I hoped it would deliver me from the deep end of the pool, from under the crushing pressure of tons of water. I agreed so I could breathe. It was resolved.

Elizabeth

* * *

NINE

Hello Anger

Hello, Anger,

It's been 291 days.

I have a weird sense of calm these days. I can't tell where it's coming from. Is it because I've confronted this trauma? It only lasts a moment at a time, but I feel different when it washes over me. The suffocation stops, and where there was once the feeling of burning, painful rage, there's now a void. This empty space feels like calmness, a feeling foreign to my mind.

The fight is over. Now it seems as though everything around me slowed down.

The heaviness in my chest has dissipated and I feel like I'm floating. It's not breathing, not thriving, since I feel stripped of all my potential, but it's like I'm barely surviving. I watched and felt myself separate, as though I became a photocopy of the person, I knew better than anyone on earth.

My previous identity is gone. I feel like my breath has left me too. I'm no longer gasping for air, and I feel calmer and more stable. I'm definitely not in control of things, but I am resigned to what's happening these days.

I am absolutely someone else, and I don't recognize me yet. Something broke in all that crying and it's like a scarcity mindset has taken over. I knew each scream in my head was costing me, each hour spent in sadness and pain was stealing from me, and I became aware of my limited breath. I'm cautious and mindful to maintain and preserve the limited breath I have. Though I'm still sinking in stress, anxiety, panic attacks, and depression, I'm sinking slowly now, less like a bag of rocks thrown in a rushing river and more like something weightless.

Sinking slowly sure beats drowning. At first, I was spiraling out of control. But now it feels like floating. Is this hope, or am I giving up? I've become aware that a part of me has died. I'm depressed, anxious, and filled with anger, but this anger feels like it's protecting me. At least it feels active and externalizes some of the pain.

Jim

* * *

Deep anger after trauma is where many victims land as they process the rage at having part of their identity taken from them. Once anonymous or private, now other people know their story. Once confident and secure in their safety, now victims feel exposed and anxious. It's completely normal to feel anger after becoming a victim. Depression and anxiety can cause people to experience a kind of rage they've never felt before. This anger can feel toxic and radioactive, but it's part of the healing process.

This is especially true because being anxious and depressed leads us to become very critical of ourselves. Over time, these uncontrollable, mean-spirited thoughts add up, leaving us even more frustrated with thoughts we feel we can't control. Anger is considered a secondary emotion, which means it's a reaction to other feelings like depression, anxiety, or confusion. Typically, we experience a primary emotion like fear, loss, or sadness first, and because these emotions create feelings of vulnerability and loss of control, they make us feel terrible. One of the ways of subconsciously trying to deal with these awful feelings is by shifting them into anger.

Anger is as important as our other primary feelings: fear, sadness, disgust, surprise, joy, and excitement. And like any of our emotions, anger is trying to tell us something. It's the mind's way of signaling that something is wrong so we can create the energy needed to address the problem by fighting, fleeing, freezing, or fawning.

For many people—especially women—anger is a dirty word. We don't feel entitled to it because we know it makes other people feel bad too. We aren't supposed to make other people feel bad, we're supposed to get along with everyone, make everyone comfortable, and keep the peace. Women don't really get to show any anger, and we pathologize women who allow this feeling to seep out. We call it "passion" in men and are very responsive to men's anger. But angry women are labeled as emotionally erratic, unstable, or radioactive when we respond naturally to the primary emotions that lead to anger.

After trauma, the red-hot wave of anger can be hard to control. It is inevitable that some of it will spill out eventually. It has to, because it's so destructive to us. This only makes our powerlessness feel more complete. We can't even control our reactions to our own feelings, which we're working so hard to contain so other people don't need to see, feel, or deal with them.

We want to feel as though this anger we're packing is fueling us toward something. But what? After trauma, we're already in so much pain, and we hope that our anger can lead to change, even just for ourselves. We hope that fighting through the shock, shame, tears, and loss of identity that follow a traumatic event will lead us somewhere. When we finally become angry and hope for some change in how our trauma is being handled, we're often re-shocked, re-shamed, and re-silenced as our anger goes ignored.

Anger drains us quickly because it keeps our body's stress responses active. Fight, flight, freeze, or fawn depletes us of all energy, attention, and ability to focus. As we become angry, our muscles tense up. Neurotransmitter chemicals are released in our brain, causing spikes in our energy, which depletes our attention and focus.

Left unprocessed, our anger becomes like a black hole for our energy. Our adrenal glands flood our bodies with stress hormones—adrenaline and cortisol, the messengers of action in our nervous systems—and the brain redirects blood away from our gut and toward our muscles in preparation for physical exertion. Right after a spike in anger, we're left drained as our system tries to regulate itself and return to a state of calm. Any of our strong emotions—even positive ones like joy and excitement—create this surge, but anger after trauma leaves us in a unique state of emotional exhaustion that makes many victims feel numb.

Anger can lead to fighting. Fighting feels like action, or at least an expression of some kind, but it is debilitating when you already feel so powerless. So as victims of trauma, we need to be aware of where our anger comes from and what it's trying to tell us so we can fight differently. Fighting differently means having a shred of control. For the first time since the dark haze of trauma surrounded us, even though we still may not be able to breathe or speak, anger can be very useful when we want to scream and shout and make the world hear us.

Anger after trauma is here to help us. It's an important part of healing, even though it's exhausting and can make victims feel yet *more* out of control. Anger is a survival mechanism. It's there to protect us, and for victims of trauma, this anger is both psychologically normal and deeply self-supportive. In these moments, anger is our friend. Where trauma steals your voice, starting to get angry about it and expressing it in healthy ways becomes a way out of the pain. Anger breaks the silence, and not a moment too soon. Getting angry can help you to heal, and healing is choosing ourselves, no matter what anyone else says or does.

Hello, Trauma,

I don't know how long it's been anymore, and I no longer care. I'm ready to heal, because you've taken up enough of my time. I realized how much tracking the date has made me lose it sometimes. I would spin, get caught up in how I was feeling, how I should be feeling, why I wasn't feeling. The madness and endless swirls of judgment need to end, so today is the day to begin.

Is healing finding happiness? Is healing letting go? Is healing working to forget, or shifting my focus? Is it just going to take more time? I don't know, but I don't want to feel this sadness and rage anymore.

Matt

* * *

TEN

Hello Self

Hello, Trauma,

It's day 62.

I'm not going to be the same after this, and losing my former self is taking a lot of energy. I'm grieving. People are telling me I'm going to come through this experience stronger, though it doesn't feel that way most of the time.

How? Why are people so sure of this? What are they talking about? Some traumas you can see, but mine is inside, making this grieving process harder.

It moves through me with scary unpredictability, shape-shifting minute by minute. Sometimes it moves fast, and I can cycle through every emotion in the blink of an eye. Other times it feels like getting stuck in one particularly painful and scary, dark place, like a record skipping on a jarring chord. I wonder if I'll find a way to express another emotion. Any other feeling has to be better.

Then there are minutes, hours, days, and maybe even weeks where it feels somewhat "under control" and I think "I beat you back, asshole. I am in charge again." But then something triggers the pain, fear, and anxiety again. maybe a nightmare or a moment of uncertainty, exhaustion, or sadness for everything that's happened. I feel like there are a few people inside me, fighting for control.

These moments feel like being dragged back into dark water and panic rises as I feel like there's nothing to hold onto. Then once again, the cycle starts up, perhaps slightly different the next time around, and I find myself free of the worst thoughts and feelings for minutes, hours, and hopefully days at a time.

I suppose this is the process of getting through trauma and trying to make sense of what's happened. I wonder if I'll ever recognize myself again.

Steph

* * *

ELEVEN

Hello Awkwardness

Hello, Trauma,

It's day 227.

I don't understand what people are saying when they try to talk to me about this. I'm just waiting, wishing, wondering what comes next. Who will say anything next? I barely know how to respond to what I'm hearing, and I can't communicate or defend myself. I'm screaming from the inside out. Outside in at this point in time. I feel like time has stopped. I'm in a permanent pause. It's like I'm playing freeze tag with the neighborhood kids, and what fun we had. The joy, laughter, screams, giggles, and occasional arguments. What a feeling, this moment of blissful interaction with my tribe. Until I'm the one tagged, and I'm frozen in place, watching everyone run by me, yelling things I can't respond to.

No one is hearing me . . . come help me, let me free. You just have to grab my hand, I will then bolt with speed and we can win the game . . . just unfreeze me. Except no one is tagging me, everyone is playing the game, and I'm here in my thoughts, waiting, wishing, wondering who will come help me . . . and then the game ends and I'm left frozen till the next time . . . wasted thoughts in the corners of my mind. But reality hits hard when I try to grab the thought—why didn't anyone say anything? Why didn't anyone help me? Why is everyone being a selfish teammate?

Why couldn't you say something? Why didn't you play the game with me? You made your own rules, or modified the game without me knowing. I didn't get that cheat code. Damn. Anger, rage, sadness—what do I feel or do with this? I understand you didn't or couldn't say anything. You didn't want to lose your own game. You matter too. Of course you do. You took care of yourself first. Just like the game of tag—don't get tagged—just run free and around. The easy, frozen teammate you can tag casually. But those frozen like me, in harder shadowed places—the frozen with risk around them—yeah, why would you save and reach out? It wasn't safe for you, so you cheered from the sidelines thinking someone else would help. Well, guess what—I'm frozen, screaming from the inside.

Frozen and Melting,

Christina

* * *

The confusing platitudes of trauma are everywhere. They're just words people say when they don't know *what* to say, which is a lot of the time. They may be well-meaning, but they suck the air out of trauma victims, because they feel inauthentic, untrustworthy, or inadequate to what we're living through. Most people are uncomfortable with inauthenticity because it's not the truth. It's not honest or real, and we know and can feel the truth when we see and hear it. Victims of trauma are living in the most acute truth, so their tolerance for inauthenticity is lower than normal. We want and need truth from other people so we can share ours.

What traumatized people need to hear isn't easy for anyone to say. But it is easy to understand why. People just don't know what to do. They're scared. But if others could acknowledge how deeply a victim feels alone, if they could understand what they're going through and could *see* them clearly, it would go a very long way. No one can ever be in our stories with us. We're alone in our heads, and no one can experience that space with us. As we stand alone in our isolation, shame, and suffocating silence, we're often waiting for the right words, some kind of opening, so we can begin to reveal our pain, exhale, and connect. The best anyone can do is empathize with us, but that's often hard for people.

Sometimes, victims hear "I'm sorry this happened to you." What's the right response to this? Thank you? That's just awkward. What are you sorry for? Victims don't feel sorry for themselves. They feel pain and fear. They don't want pity. They want action and support and acknowledgment. They want change, not the condolences we reserve for life's minor inconveniences or something beyond any human control.

Unfortunately, "Sorry" doesn't go as far as we wish it would. A victim may want to reply: "Thank you for being sorry, but what are you going to do about it? Is sorry a replacement for action?'" If we're just sorry, does that mean we're okay with this kind of thing happening again? Sorry does very little if it has no movement behind it, and it rarely does. Our sympathy says, "I'm sorry," whereas our empathy says, "I'm hurting with you." Sorry keeps all responsibility at a distance, as though there's nothing anyone can do to protect people from harm or reform environments where trauma occurs.

Sorry leaves people feeling isolated, falling into a strange space in which people feel *something*, but they won't join a victim in the space they occupy. They don't want to go all in, go all the way to empathy, because whatever the victim feels—sadness, anger, fear, anxiety—might rub off on them. This is confusing and leaves victims more silent and less able to connect. What would actually help would be hearing "I am so angry this happened to you." This moves the needle. Victims *are* angry it happened, so where is everyone else's anger?

Sorry gives people an excuse to say "I've acknowledged your pain," but they don't have to touch it. They don't have to feel a thing or get into the mess of sadness and pain. They don't have to *do* anything. They don't have to admit that there's a problem or a massive systemic issue that allows people to be harmed, silenced, and forgotten. Anger, however, is action. It's motivating. It means we won't accept these conditions, and we will try to change them. Anger gets people moving together. It leads us to protect each other. It identifies a danger, works to contain it, and it *collaborates*. It speaks and screams, and we can all hear it. We can all *feel* it. Sorry, on the other hand, whispers. It maintains the status quo, and after a quick mention of it, we can all move on.

Our standard go-to expressions are missing the empathetic connection which makes victims feel protected, seen, and understood. Getting on the same emotional pathway with them means exploring how they're *actually* doing, even though there may be some discomfort and it may take time. What we can do instead of expressing "Sorry" is find out what emotional range a victim is in, so *they* can connect with *us*. Victims can be anywhere along the continuum, and it may be very intense for them that day. But when you find out where *they* are, you can connect with them there instead of asking them to come to your emotional domain to get the connection they so desperately need as they try to heal.

The most comforting questions and comments are along the lines of: "How are you really doing?" or "I don't want to assume how you're feeling, but please know I'm here and you can talk if you want to." This allows victims to feel as though a safe connection is available to them. It allows someone to talk, if they want to, or just share space with you. It creates an environment of acknowledgment that, yes, something happened, and you are all in to listen, talk, and truly be there with them, when they're ready.

A space as open and honest as this allows victims to guide the depth they're comfortable diving to, with you beside them. It lets them just breathe. It assures them you're there for whatever frequency they choose, as you're just the passenger helping them find meaning as they heal. It may take time for someone to open up or trust that you're genuinely there to understand without judgment. But keep showing up. Give them space and allow some room for everyday normalcy within the shared space of healing. Just be present. Victims will oscillate between pain and normalcy, and it's hard for anyone to manage their feelings with so much emotional whiplash.

In a similar vein, victims get a lot of blank stares. This forces them into the position of reassuring whoever is staring that they're okay, they don't have to occupy the space of the traumatic experience, feel any of the anger or discomfort, or even connect at all. The blank stare says, "Hey, I don't have the emotional capacity to go there, so I'm going to do nothing. I don't have the words that need to be said, so I will say nothing. I'm just going to take care of myself."

This makes sense, and it's part of our collective response to so much trauma around us. We freeze rather than address it directly. It's often not ill-intended, but it's all most people are capable of. But for victims, it's hard to navigate the silent stares and shifty body language and not feel invisible or get the message that "I don't want to help. I don't care about you." This hurts, and makes a victim feel like an exposed, raw nerve, naked for everyone to see.

It's hard to realize that often someone is just communicating that they don't know what to do, and they're waiting for the victim to tell them how to interact and engage. This can feel like hard work, but it's genuinely not about any victim of trauma. It's about someone else's emotional paralysis, not ours. Since most people don't know how to respond to trauma, conflict, unhappiness, or any negative emotion, they're going to hide from it. It's the most common reaction: freezing in response to someone else's pain.

Sometimes appropriate physical touch, like extending a hand, helps because physical connection releases oxytocin in our bodies and spreads the endorphins of care, empathy, and calm through us. It promotes positive emotions, indicates we're really present, and means we're focused on the person we're speaking with. It says we're showing up authentically and sharing space in a meaningful way. It takes making eye contact one step further and communicates acknowledgment. It means I see and hear you, and as small as it seems, it really works on our brains. It grounds people together to stop what they're doing and says, "Hey, I am here with you. I see you and hear you, even if talking feels too hard."

When someone asks, "What can I do to help?" trauma victims may feel overwhelmed, because there isn't an easy answer. Our minds cycle between "Get as angry as I have been," "Protect other people," and "I have no idea," but none of these are easy to say. What we *want* to say is "Let's take action together to make sure everyone feels safe and can be vulnerable. Let's lift the cone of silence that keeps people trapped and let's make sure no one feels the isolation I do." But that's a lot. There's a time and place for this much of a response, and if were honest, most people are not prepared to hear those statements, let alone do anything about them. They just become unspoken words, with limited action, and continued trapped pain and isolation.

These normal, natural, and everyday questions are like a minefield for victims of trauma. Although they may be the most sincere engagement we've ever heard, asked by people who really care and really want to help, they don't allow a victim much room to maneuver. We swallow our real answers because we're living in pain. It's clear that these efforts to connect are hard. What we need is to expand our emotional vocabulary so we can talk about hard things.

But we don't practice talking about how we feel, in nearly all environments, so we're under-skilled at asking the right questions and finding honest answers. We default to simple words to explain complex feelings. We don't teach people how to identify their feelings, so they never have to practice articulating what's on their minds. It makes us unable to pick up how *others* feel and leaves each of us more isolated and more silent than we need to be.

Think about it like this: before a baby can speak, they can already feel their emotions, and those of their caregivers, but they can't communicate them verbally. Then, they learn the words and develop the ability to identify, read, and respond to emotions in other people, as they begin to form connections. But as adults, we blunt this knowledge, partly to protect ourselves and partly because we can't express our feelings in every environment. Without the opportunity or vocabulary, we slow down feeling our own feelings, and we stop consciously identifying feelings in other people.

This makes building and maintaining healthy, safe, and secure connections harder and harder. It also means we're unable to respond appropriately to how other people are feeling, which contributes to our culture of psychological unsafety.

The only cure is real, honest, vulnerable, and sincere communication that shines light on what's really happening.

* * *

Hello, Trauma,

It's day 310.

I know people want me to be better, and they wanted that yesterday. But I can't go faster than I am. I can only do what I can, one step at a time. I have heard it suggested that I should "just get over it already," so I can get back to what and who I was. But this has nothing to do with me. It's what other people want and think they need in order to feel comfortable with events outside their control.

Controlling myself is hard enough. How am I going to be able to control anyone else? I can't. I am doing the best I can. Trauma has its own schedule and I'm just along for the ride while my brain works consciously and subconsciously to do what it needs, for me and for us.

Chelsea

* * *

TWELVE

Hello Healing

Hello, Me.

It's day 402.

Exhale, breathe . . . pause . . . reflect . . . what is this feeling? Calm, serenity. A milestone moment. A smile on my face and a pep in my step as I am coming back online. I am lighter, I have energy, I have a controlled, calmer flame burning inside. But the flame is not burning me from the inside. No, this is different, yet familiar. This flame is small and warm, letting me glow on the outside. Small, radiant energy—belief, hope, commitment to connect. I am home. Not physically sleeping in a bed home, but my work home. Work feels like home. I feel accepted, wanted, needed, valued, connected. I feel I belong, but more importantly, I feel calm, safe, curious.

This isn't the honeymoon phase of a new job—this is family. This is home. This is a foundation of growth and building together. I could challenge this and seek the cracks. They are there—any place has them. But the foundation is strong. I am here, helping build this and we are making this a welcoming home. I have found my home, or my home has found me . . . goodness me . . .

Sam

* * *

As oversimplified as it sounds, after trauma, pivoting our minds and bodies toward health *is* healing. It means doing the things necessary to promote and preserve our health, even though they're harder than ever when trauma takes control. For most of us, this means healthy food, exercise, rest, calm, quiet, peace, security, music, safety, and close connections, even if it's just connection to ourselves. It means giving ourselves a break from the spin cycle of thinking and feeling so much.

I know these are just words. But they're also *actions* and our actions lead to changes in us. They're how we make trauma make *some* sense, because in our first responses, we can't make sense of anything. These words work to try to reframe our thinking so we can stop judging ourselves, stop feeling shame and anger, stop isolating ourselves, and stop living in silence.

We heal by learning to navigate the new space we live in rather than constantly reaching for the person we used to be because we don't recognize ourselves. It means working hard to be less reactive by nature, to respond differently, to be patient and compassionate with ourselves, to tend to the wounds of our minds and hearts. It's exactly what we would try to do for someone else. This will never *not* be a process. It will always be a wound we must tend to, and we will have to get used to this reality.

The truth victims often need to force themselves to confront is that we don't think we'll ever be *fully* healed because we don't ever want other people to forget what happened or forget about us. We can't forget it ourselves. We can heal up to a point, but we're someone new now, someone who carries the trauma with them. Victims may go hours, days, or weeks without thinking about their experience. But they will feel it again, especially if they see or hear of someone else's traumatic experience. Though we may be through the darkest parts of our own trauma, painful and destructive things happen to other people, all around us, every day. Their experiences remind us of our own when we least expect it, and we may be totally unprepared to be thrown backwards. When this happens, it can feel like we're stuck, but it's a natural part of the process of recovery.

Self-doubt begins to creep into our minds and test our security and safety as we begin to really heal. It challenges us by whispering "Are you really safe? Remember that one time you thought you were, and you were wrong? Do you recall how dark it was? Can you trust your judgment of really being safe now?" While you're healing from trauma and re-accepting yourself, you begin to doubt your surroundings and yourself, everywhere. This is our mind's way of protecting our hearts, because we never want to feel that kind of pain again. This, too, is a natural part of the healing process, like testing the ground to ensure it can support you.

Healing is like learning to walk again. It's a period of being emotionally tentative with ourselves, like exposing a new scar to sunlight. It takes time to allow our mind to integrate the ground we've covered, and to trust that we can be comfortable in our own minds and bodies again. Like everything else, it's a process, and it goes slowly. We may not realize how much we've grown until we feel our strength coming back. But it's happening beneath the surface of our consciousness, which is working around the clock to take care of us. Healing virtually always happens, because our brains want us to live.

Healing is living. Healing is taking tender, active, honest care of our wounds. Healing is forgiving and accepting ourselves without judgment, shame, or anger. Healing is getting our voices back so we can speak and listen. But it's also caring for ourselves out loud, publicly, and for all to see and hear.

* * *

Hello, Reader,

I want to check in with you for a moment, and have you check in with yourself. The journal entries throughout this book were a deliberate tool to assist you in tapping into the emotional breadth of trauma, what it feels like, how it can control someone's mind, and alter how they show up in the world. This is such a complicated and personal topic that it can be hard to even share with yourself. I am grateful you are taking time to lean in, learn, heal, and help make change.

I'm grateful to the people out there who have shared their experiences with trauma to help name the feelings so many struggle with, because trauma is a part of our lives and it's everywhere. Chances are, most of us here have experienced some kind of trauma, though we may not call it that.

I hear you, I see you, and I am here. I know you're there and I know what you're going through. We may never talk about it, but I understand. Though trying to fight your way through trauma is possibly the loneliest journey you'll ever take, silently walking alongside you is everyone else who has experienced the depth of this acute pain and all the confusion that comes with it. We're in every building, every store, on the street, in doctors' offices, on the bus, train, sitting in traffic with you, in our homes, at work, and on every team we faithfully follow. This is why we need to change. Because there are so many of us.

We may be putting a brave face on what's going on under the surface, but we're all here, each at a different stage of trying, hoping, praying, and working to feel better, or at least feel less pain. We are working hard to avoid boiling over, lashing out, or completely shutting down. Mostly, we are living in silence. This is bad for us, and for everyone.

Even if you feel as though you're numb and something inside you died, you are somewhere in the process. I won't call it "recovery," because that's patronizing and insensitive. Recovery sounds like you'll just get over it or wake up one day and be fine. Not great, not better than ever, just fine. Sometimes it's just about understanding your experience, since "recovery" seems like an impossible mountain to climb.

Perhaps, like me, you're in a new reality, in which you live with this inside you, everywhere you go. It's not something you chose to carry, but here it is. And today, we're all trying to re-assemble the parts of us that feel shattered, enraged, scared, shocked, confused, sick, ashamed, compartmentalized, hurt, and traumatized.

I won't say "It gets better," though I believe it does. Instead: there is hope and there is a future in which this feels less painful. Hope that comes from knowing you're not alone in your feelings. I am hoping with you and hoping for you, and together we can change our culture of silence, our shame, blame, and our tolerance of the traumas we go through.

I'm honored to be a voice of change for those who suffer in silence. More importantly, I'm passionate about making systemic change in our environments so others can feel safe, secure, and thrive.

So thank you for reading those entries. But you're about to open a new diary of change, of culture, and of making wrongs right.

Take a breath and continue to dive into my ideas for how we can address and make meaning of the trauma in our lives, how we can create more safety, security, and understanding when trauma does happen.

—Dr. C

THIRTEEN

Something's Wrong around Here

There's something wrong about how the culture of sport operates. Unintentionally, we're harming people in athletics. We're creating emotional and psychological trauma, but we have a chance to fix it. We have a responsibility to fix it, because sport is one of our most powerful opportunities to connect with others and foster health, community, and a culture of care. This doesn't mean taking our eyes off the ball, losing championships, or completely changing what we're there to do. It means winning, but with better emotional and psychological skills. It means winning as a *consequence* of a culture of care, which will benefit everyone in our community.

Sport participation can have so many meaningful benefits to our personal development, in spite of a culture that can be problematic. Athletics can improve our mental, physical, and emotional well-being. It can teach us how to push our bodies physically to improve technical and tactical skills in a competitive environment.

Through sport participation, people can increase their endurance, strength, flexibility, and overall physical fitness. The regular exercise can help reduce the risk of chronic diseases such as heart disease, diabetes, and obesity. But athletes are not joining sport thinking about the long-lasting impact on their physical well-being. They're joining because the pull of sport is irresistible, and many of us want to be part of a culture that creates heroes. We join because it's our passion and our purpose, and there's nowhere we would rather be.

Among the many benefits we get from our participation is socialization, fun, an opportunity to use our energy in healthy ways, being part of a team, learning new skills, being immersed in an activity, and challenging ourselves. Fun is essential for long-term engagement in sport, and the positive aspects of sport breed an opportunity for everyone to learn personal growth and improve their life skills across domains. Lessons like goal setting, communication, leadership, managing our emotions, handling pressure, problem solving, a strong work ethic, and the sheer pleasure of competing are all positive outcomes of sport that can't be underestimated.

A point of debate though, is: does sport build character or not? I've always believed that it does strengthen and enhance our character and innate characteristics. But *what* character is built depends on the environment an athlete is in. Each environment teaches athletes how to think, act, feel, and be in the world in different ways. The character building that comes with athletics is a function of the culture of their team and its values, and that varies enormously. And as we know, some environments are healthier than others.

One component of sport participation that gets less attention than it should is how it impacts our emotional wellness. Moving our bodies has the potential to significantly impact our mental health in the best ways. Exercise releases endorphins, which are hormones that help reduce stress and anxiety levels, improve mood, and promote better sleep. Through sport participation, we can also learn to manage stress, build self-confidence, and develop a positive attitude that extends to every part of our lives. But to reap these benefits, we need more environments where we can build our mental wellness through mental skills training and develop essential skills like focus and resilience. This requires a culture of care that balances all aspects of sport to create the strongest athletes, teams, and individuals.

Sport is an outcome-based activity. It's about wins and losses, and we love to win. I've never met a person who says, "I can't wait to lose today," because we just aren't wired that way. Winning comes with an addictive thrill, and building and refining the competitor in us can become all-consuming. We build and train athletes to earn championships. We love to excel at our trade, and we work harder, giving more and more of ourselves to become winners and champions. This is what we value, right? But should it be the *only* thing we value?

Today, sport culture is in a crisis across the board. This is particularly true for youth sport, which has become toxic and traumatic for young athletes, teaching many of the wrong lessons. What's wrong with the youth athletics culture is not the players. It's the entire system that fails to support kids, turning up the volume on anxiety, depression, and poor mental health, instead of helping to develop healthy self-esteem and self-image. Coaches are condescending and often scream when showing their disappointment. Aggressive parents are harsh judges and openly display anger at their kids' performance. A relentless drive to win and the crazy pressure we're putting on children to succeed is the opposite of what young people need, and it's the opposite of psychological safety and security. Kids need support, care, and encouragement to learn and grow, instead of building champions fixated on one goal. With a culture of care, though, we can build allies to assist one another in thriving, both within sport and in the rest of our lives.

The current culture is not a culture of care, but an environment of hostility and fear that causes unnecessary stress. So, it's no surprise that 70 to 80 percent of young athletes drop out of team sport by thirteen to fifteen years of age, according to a recent examination on youth sport.

Young athletes are having bad experiences with their coaches and feeling extreme pressure from their parents—both their own and their teammates'. Parents are the leading factor in the development of self-esteem in kids, and when parents use their influence to stress the importance of winning at all costs, mental health be damned, it erodes kids' self-image. Children who experience this kind of pressure on a regular basis abandon sport to protect themselves. They're also more prone to developing mental and physical health problems in the short and longer term.

Sport has stopped being fun for young athletes in large part because adult coaches and parents are unable to control their emotions from the sidelines. Their sole focus is on the outcome rather than the effort, team building, and healthy collaboration that attracts young athletes in the first place. Coaching through intimidation and negativity is destroying our kids' confidence, and the aggression being transmitted is dangerous. Instead of "toughening" or inspiring children, this kind of bullying and pressure is hurting kids at an important stage in the development of their identity. We would call this abuse in any other context, but we tolerate it in athletics. Why do we accept burning out and harming children this way? Isn't this the opposite of teaching people how to be happy and healthy, psychologically safe and secure as part of a culture of care?

This bracketed morality of sport—think of it like a moral pause—is a big part of the problem. The culture of athletics suspends the usual moral obligation to consider the needs of everyone involved, as though we're ignoring right and wrong, in pursuit of a win. We accept less mature or moral behavior from athletes and sport organizations than we would from anyone else. But lowering our morality and standards of protection to pursue athletic success comes at a real cost. It can lead to athletes displaying antisocial behavior on and off the field, controlling and aggressive coaches, and an entire culture that lives outside the bounds of what we consider morally acceptable behavior. Yet we tolerate it. It's not just that sport culture is toxic behind the scenes. It's spilling out into public all the time.

This is the most damaging aspect of the culture of youth sport: the way we allow other adults—like coaches—to speak to our kids. The way we sweep things under the rug by minimizing the inhumane actions of organizations or people that have verbally abused kids is unacceptable. Sure, there are fines and the occasional suspension, but this isn't real accountability. Real accountability means we won't accept or teach this aggression, ever.

But if youth sport is experiencing a crisis of unhealthy culture, adult sport is in an altogether different league of toxicity and trauma. The issues run the gamut from harassment, abuse, cheating, doping, player misconduct, gun violence, drugs, spousal and child abuse, gambling, driving under the influence, spying on opposing teams, overt racism, corruption, sex scandals, youth athlete sexual abuse, grooming minors, serial sexual molestation, and on, and on and on. And these are only the stories that make it into mainstream news. There are likely more incidents that are never reported or are "resolved" quietly. Clearly, sport has a problem with trauma, violence, sexual assault, and what the culture allows to go unchecked. For the victims, there is no resolution.

The mental toll of toxic sport culture is bleeding out, partly because a champion is taught to be strong, stoic, relentless, fearless, aggressive, and uncomplaining. It's also because we tolerate problems we shouldn't. We embrace behavior that becomes dangerous and leads to traumatic dominance rather than working to change it.

But why? We teach athletes to remove their emotions and mask their feelings, to remain silent about what hurts and harms them, and to focus on one thing: winning, regardless of how it may affect their mental health. We tell them it's part of the deal and to suck it up, because that's what winners do. Our champion athletes are taught what it takes to win and how they should feel and act. This is the cognitive dissonance in sport; there is much more to any athlete, coach, or team than just winning.

This is changing, slowly. But when we make changing the culture of sport our priority and focus on mental health, not just mental toughness, we'll see faster results.

Sport has a history of courageous voices who have worked to change how we talk about mental health, including Michael Phelps, former competitive swimmer and the most decorated Olympic athlete of all time, who said, "Therapy saved my life." And NBA basketball player Kevin Love, who said, "What I have found about mental health and mental illness is that it takes many shapes and forms . . . the demographic I really want to point out and look to is children. I think it is very important for kids and their parents to understand what is going on . . ." And Brandon Marshall, a former NFL wide receiver, who said, "The dumb mistakes I've made in college, the stupid things I've said in the media. All of that led to me sitting down with my team, my agent, and my assistant at the time and saying, 'It's time to get help and not just talk therapy, but let's figure out if there's a program out there'." And professional track and field sprinter Noah Lyles, who said, "Recently, I decided to get on antidepressant medication. That was one of the best decisions I have made in a while . . . Thank you God for mental health."

And Hayden Hurst, tight end for the Carolina Panthers, who said, "There's this persona that you're an NFL player and you're almost a robot . . . but I think it's more masculine to truly reach out for help and say 'Hey, I have a problem and I need assistance here'." And retired gymnast and two-time Olympian Aly Raisman, who said, "My results, or my worth in the sport, is based on what other people think of me . . . I'm still trying to navigate how to fully recover, but I've learned the importance of being kind to myself . . . I'm sure . . . anyone can relate to experiencing some kind of trauma or anxiety, can recognize just how exhausting it can be."

And Michael Oher, former NFL offensive tackle, who said, "I'm still traumatized and I still deal with things that I dealt with as a kid. If you're still dealing with trauma, [therapy] is definitely needed early on, because I had to do that to get back healthy. The mind is the most powerful thing and it has to be healthy to be successful. I bottled so much stuff up throughout my life. I carried that with me, and I think it hurt me in the long run. That may be the only thing holding you back from being where you want to be—talking to somebody."

These athletes—and many others who have spoken publicly about the importance of their mental health in recent years—are changing the sport culture and how we define strength. Athletes play the role of hero to many and represent an idealization of what strong is. They are starting to take a stand to make mental and emotional health a foundational component of athletics. They're shifting the narrative about mental health at work and bringing focus to the dynamics that pose threats to athletes, including the relentless pressure to attain perfection, the pressure of being in the public eye, and being taught to win at all costs.

But in spite of the work being done by some to bring mental wellness into the conversation about sport, our toxic culture is still sometimes critical of athletes who publicly prioritize their mental health, or even mention that mental health is part of their lives at all. Look at the backlash against Olympic gymnast Simone Biles and professional tennis player Naomi Osaka, who both stepped back from the highest level of competition in their sport to focus on what they needed in the moment: to protect and care for themselves because they needed *care* and *protection* from the pressure of being superhero athletes.

Some people could relate deeply with their vulnerability and honesty. For others it was like kryptonite. Some people called them "lazy" and "entitled," as though they were *not* entitled to mental health or were required to perform for the world, regardless of how bad they were feeling. The expectation that an athlete should bury their natural, human feelings—even feelings of weakness—is not only wrong and destructive, it's immoral. It tells everyone watching—especially young people—that how an athlete feels doesn't matter. This actively discourages people from examining their own feelings of fear or anxiety and instead encourages silence.

We've all seen Simone and Naomi display strength and remarkable athletic skills, but why should we believe that's *all* they are? That they aren't complete, full humans, with stress, anxiety, fear, and distress too? Why would we demand only what we want to see from them—the exceptional—without acknowledging their humanity too? Who are we to cherry pick among our superhero athletes' normal, human characteristics, shunning them for being human when they need to take care of themselves?

The shame that comes from putting oneself first, after a lifetime of training that says "Push through everything that hurts" is part of why these two athletes' courage was so important. Simone said it perfectly: "It's okay sometimes to even sit out the big competitions to focus on yourself, because it shows how strong of a competitor and person that you really are, rather than just battle through it."

Her statement captures how the pressure to perform can turn toxic and overwhelming. Coaches and parents can't see, or choose to ignore, what this pressure is doing to kids. So the more elite athletes are able to voice their struggles with the pressure they're facing, the easier it is for others to join them in speaking up about their own mental health. This can have a significant impact on our young athletes, who often leave athletics because of these stresses and pressures. These two women—and the many other athletes who advocate for the importance of mental health in sport—are the champions our young athletes need, because so often, coaches and parents can't or aren't hearing and seeing what the stress and pressure to perform is doing to kids.

By putting their own psychological safety and security front and center, these mental health advocates and change-makers are leading the transformation of the toxic culture of sport. Their courage cuts through the narrative of "win at all costs" and gets to the core of real athletic excellence: mental health is as important as physical health. Sport is about challenging ourselves, but that shouldn't make it impossible to keep track of what's important, and mental health is as important as physical health.

We can't see when our mental health is out for a few games due to injury. It can't be worn in a cast or brace, but being unable to see it doesn't mean it isn't there. Anxiety, depression, and emotional exhaustion *are* injuries, and deserve to be treated as carefully as sprains and torn ligaments.

Think about what "win at all costs" really means. It doesn't leave much room for values and ethical standards. Just look at the growing list of scandals, criminal charges, hurt, burnt out, silenced, and traumatized people born of an environment that only sees success in terms of wins and losses. These people are casualties of a system that needs to change.

This isn't a "performance mindset." It's sport culture's *fixed* mindset that tells us it "has to be this way," or "this is what works to win." It doesn't have to be this way and it isn't working. It's damaging, unethical, and destructive. We can re-envision success through a different lens, one that's more conscious of human experience, including the mental wellness of our teams and our entire culture.

FOURTEEN

Trauma Is on Every Team; Our Athletes Are Not Okay

My first experience of living within sport's culture of champions was in 1992. I was in Louisiana, without my parents and with my track and field family. We were about to compete in the biggest championship of my life. It was the Junior Olympics, and I was running the 1500 meter, which is nearly a mile, on nine-year-old legs.

It was a hot, muggy, swampy kind of day. My heart was racing, but I put on my sweatpants to go warm up in the 105-degree heat. My coach had a rule that we always had to wear our sweatpants when we warmed up, so I did as I was told, regardless of the heat and humidity. I always did what the coach told me to do. I was a kid trying to perform for my parents and coaches, like almost every other nine-year-old athlete I know. I was going to follow his rules, no matter how uncomfortable I felt.

So, I warmed up, sweating, and I couldn't breathe. My heart was racing as we got in line to go race, like a herd of little cattle. I was following along, doing what everyone else was doing, but I was scared. Like frozen scared. I recall looking around thinking, "Geez, all these kids look really fast." I was becoming more overwhelmed and anxious and I felt the stress rising in me. Even though my teammates were around me, I felt completely alone. Then all of a sudden, I felt a large hand press down on my shoulder.

My whole body tightened up. I looked up and heard, "Hey, Hill, how are you doing?" I took a big, deep breath. It was my coach. *My* coach. He had coached me for years and I loved him. He was smart, strong, and a little scary, but I trusted him. I believed in him and wanted to make him proud. He was building champions, and there I was at age nine, in the biggest championship of my life. I felt the impact of this moment and responded to him accordingly.

"I'm good, Coach."

I was *not* good. Very much the opposite. But I wasn't about to tell him that I was scared, overwhelmed, and lost, since that would show weakness and I'd be a failure. He put his hand on my back and said, "It's gonna be all right, kid. You got a lot of heart."

Got a lot of heart. I didn't even know what it meant, but I said it to myself over and over again. I didn't realize it back then, but that moment at age nine was going to shape who I was during that race, for the rest of my athletic endeavors, and the person I would become. It's the crux of my philosophy of who I am as a mother, a professional, and a member of the community of sport. It's the lens through which I reexamine the culture of champions through a culture of care.

I didn't know what my coach's words meant at first, but I knew that what I needed from him at that moment was *care,* which we all need. I needed him to see me and give me the reassurance of his attention so I could feel that I wasn't alone. That he had my back. But I had an inkling that having a lot of heart really *meant* something. Something important. It suggested caring in a *real* way. Really seeing and hearing people and connecting with them in scary moments, when they're looking around for someone to connect with, even for a second. Now I know what having a lot of heart means. It's acting with feeling, living with passion, caring for yourself and others in the shared pursuit of a goal, and having love for and belief in the people around you, even when it's hard. This is exactly what a culture of care is and does for people. It's leading with our hearts.

Fast forward a few years, and the message of "Bury your feelings. Do as you're told. Don't show emotions. Just suck it up and run," was how I understood my job as an athlete. This led to a lot of success for me, and I won a lot of races. I had visions of competing at the Division One level. I was successful in the sense that I had a lot of wins, and I had the medals and accolades to show for it, but winning wasn't fun for me. It was the opposite.

My adolescent brain couldn't understand how winning and being a champion didn't feel the way I thought it was supposed to. Wasn't it supposed to be fun? Wasn't I doing it right? Wasn't winning the goal? I was lost and confused, but I continued to chase the next championship because that's what you do as an athlete. That's the constant message young athletes get: be better, be the best, work harder. If you don't, someone else will.

Isn't that what sport and life are all about? Pushing through discomfort to achieve the goal? My confusion and feelings of uncertainty grew. I didn't know how to feel in this culture of championship building. I didn't know how to talk about my feelings. Winners don't talk about their doubts, so I didn't talk about mine. I kept them bottled up. There's nothing healthy about that silence, even the self-imposed kind.

I kept telling myself that I could not fail. I focused on what I knew, which was how to work hard, be a good athlete, and keep chasing championships. But no one asked me how I was *feeling*, and I couldn't have told them if they did. They asked me how I was *doing*, which is not the same. And if they did ask? I would have just replied "Good." My world had taught me that champions are strong, not weak, and feelings of being lost and scared are not champion qualities.

This is where sport fails competitors early in their lives by sending the wrong message about feelings. The brain is rapidly developing, creating the emotional framework as an adolescent is exploring and making meaning of their world. They're trying to understand their emotions, the emotions of their friends, parents, family members, and their coaches. Emotions are complicated, and it's easy for anyone to get those feelings wrong. In a stressful environment like competition, the brain is even more vulnerable to emotional outbursts and breakdowns.

Because the adolescent brain's frontal lobe—which controls expressions of language, judgment and our ability to self-monitor—is not fully developed, our athletes are wandering around their youth trying hard to navigate their complicated and sometimes overwhelming emotions without much, if any, guidance. This is a crucial time to help their brain development through a culture of care in sport. We're missing this window to create champions who can balance their minds and bodies so they can thrive and excel across the domains of their lives.

Young athletes are in an identity-formation stage of development, with an increased range of hormonal changes, which affect their emotional regulation. They're shifting from a potentially selfless nature to a more ego-centric, self-focused mindset, as adolescent athletes shift from playing for their coach or parent to learning to intrinsically play for themselves. This happens while trying to navigate a tricky period in which they're figuring out self-identity, self-formation, and self-worth.

This stage of growth and development, when people are learning to like themselves and be in the world with everyone else, comes at a time when being the best at something fuels their developing ego. It's easy to see how getting praised and being rewarded for winning, and being taught that their value is *only* in their wins, can become their entire identity.

The problem is, we rarely help young athletes navigate the pressures of winning or how to deal with the fear of failure and the fear of constant evaluation that will always be a part of sport. We miss the opportunity to teach young athletes self-care and the building of self, no matter if they win or lose, receive praise or accolades, or not. This can set them up for emotional roadblocks later in life. But a culture of care can help manage the ups and downs, the wins and losses.

It's our job as adults to help them navigate their emotional world. Since we don't, we end up with adult athletes who are under-skilled at understanding their emotional landscape, who remain silent about how they're feeling when they face a serious issue. That can lead to trouble, for them and for the people in their lives. When we don't have access to our inner emotional landscape, it creates friction in our lives. Friction leads to conflict. Conflict can lead to aggression, and aggression can destroy some relationships and cause trauma in others. It keeps us inaccessible to ourselves, and hard to reach and connect with other people. This eats away at our mental health and well-being and makes it hard to find happiness. And it really takes the fun out of sport.

Sport has adopted a confusing mixed message in an effort to address this unhealthy culture: "It's okay to not be okay." These words contain a lot of meaning, like "it's been resolved, " but they bury layers of complexity. In theory, it means that just because someone's not doing well doesn't mean they have to act like everything's fine. But this implies we think it's wrong to feel bad mentally or emotionally, and that it's really bad to show it or tell anyone.

It's strange that we've built so many barriers to being honest about how we feel that we need a reminder to be human. "It's okay to not be okay" is the shorthand we've come up with to remind ourselves that having human emotions and being honest about them is normal. This idea would be great if we fostered environments that teach us how to feel, and especially, how to feel when we fail, feel weak, sad, depressed, lonely, upset, or when we lose. Not only is it okay to not feel okay, it's *essential*.

An emotional response to an abnormal situation *is* normal. An emotional response to emotional pain or anxiety and the stress of the enormous public pressure to win *is* healthy. It means someone is actually present, paying attention, and our brains are taking in what's going on around us. Remaining stoic and pretending we're fine is the *real* abnormal response. Hiding pain is only a temporary solution, because eventually it leaks out around us through aggression, violence, and dysfunction, and potentially creates trauma in other people. Since we can't pick and choose among the emotions we experience, we're transmitting the wrong message to people around us when we suppress our normal responses to problems in our environment. It's not only our *own* feelings we're burying. When other people aren't okay, we want them to be silent about it too. There is nothing normal, healthy, or psychologically safe and secure in this standard.

Our physical health is intimately intertwined with our mental health. Burying negative emotions like anxiety, depression, and anger causes stress on our physical bodies. It can disrupt the function of our stress hormones and increases our risk of developing chronic illness as our immune system becomes exhausted. Our minds and bodies aren't separate entities, though we often treat them that way. A champion's physical body can't excel when the mind is being ignored.

FIFTEEN

Sport Is What We *Do*, Not Who We *Are*

My kids say it best when they explain what I do: "Mama teaches people how to be happy." What a simple and powerful statement. I teach athletes and coaches how to feel their feelings and manage their emotions so they can be more successful, but also *happier*, in sport and in the rest of their lives. I teach them that sport is what they *do*, not who they *are*. I help them understand themselves in body and mind. I want them to love what they do, and I hope it does make them happy, but I try to put it in the proper context: as part of their lives, but not their entire identity. Being a champion is great, but it pales in comparison to being emotionally well, stable, and happy. We can learn to be happy, but we rarely have the chance to strengthen these skills.

Happiness is an emotion like any other, and we often get it wrong. It's not uncommon for people to think that sometimes, we'll just wake up happy, like we got lucky. It doesn't work that way. Like any goal we set for ourselves, it takes consistent hard work to achieve. It requires commitment and focus. It means developing the emotional and social skills that support our happiness. The way to strengthen these muscles and become emotionally well starts with the practice of self-awareness, taking perspective, empathy, emotional regulation, and social skills that support happiness and connection.

When we focus on learning to be happy, we develop the ability to check in with ourselves, which helps us identify what fuels us and what drains us. We learn how to manage and navigate our emotions. We become able to connect with others in ways that are meaningful both intrinsically and extrinsically. And we continue to make space to care for ourselves in *all* aspects of our lives.

Once we've done the work to put this healthy framework in place, it's not like we can set it and forget it. Sustained emotional wellness requires maintenance. That doesn't mean we're going to be happy 100 percent of the time. But we can have stability and a sense of balance in our lives—in our relationships, our jobs, and with ourselves. We will always need to return to the practice of self-awareness, but once we've learned to do this, our growth continues.

Life demands that we pour ourselves into certain areas at times and minimize or neglect other areas of ourselves—like, we can't go to work and also spend the day daydreaming or unfocused on the task at hand. True balance and emotional wellness mean checking in and taking time to care for yourself when your batteries are running low.

For athletes, performers, or any high achiever, if we only pour energy into maximum optimization and success, it doesn't take long before we drain that battery (and all others). We become burned out, overworked, and apathetic. This leads to unhealthy habits and a total lack of balance in the other areas of our lives. Sport isn't just physical, it's also mental and emotional, using both our heads and our hearts. Our thoughts influence our actions, and our actions influence our thoughts. That's why it's important to understand our thoughts and feelings, because where the mind goes, the body follows, and vice versa.

According to National Institute of Mental Health, it is estimated that one in five adults in the United States experiences mental illness in a given year. That same data point is true for adolescents. One in five thirteen- to eighteen-year-olds will experience mental illness in a year, which is a number so high, it should scare us.

If a basketball coach has a team of fifteen players, at least three of them are experiencing mental illness at every practice. It means more than just having a bad day. The players may be there in body, but their minds are probably somewhere else. They're going through the motions. They may feel distracted, sad, hurt, depressed, or angry. The point is, they're in pain but they're hiding it.

Sport can also become an escape from emotional turmoil for an athlete who is struggling deeply in isolation at home. And we wouldn't know, because their athletic performance may not be suffering. The mask of mental illness is real, and many people are wearing it.

When an athlete experiences a physical injury, a team of medical professionals is deployed to ensure a quick recovery. But when an athlete experiences a psychological injury, the sport community often looks the other way. It can amplify an athlete's feelings of loneliness and abandonment to the mix, since they may feel like there is nowhere to turn for help.

The pressure of our performance environment is causing more psychological symptoms to present in athletes. Recent studies in mental health and athletes estimated 33 percent of college students report significant mental health symptoms, and 35 percent of elite professional athletes suffer from mental health concerns but only 10 to 15 percent of them are seeking help for their emotional problems. Far more struggle on a regular basis and tell no one, because of the stigma that needing help weakens them, taught to them by our culture of unflinching warriors. Thirty percent of our athletes report feeling psychological symptoms like overtraining, sleep disturbances, changes in eating habits, isolation, overthinking, loss of enjoyment in activities, and being overwhelmed on a daily basis. These numbers only reflect the athletes' voices that are strong enough to speak out and to seek help. This is one of the areas where the culture of sport can make the biggest change. We can make mental health training and support a core value of our culture.

There's no doubt that sport can promote prosocial behavior in young people as they learn how to be part of a team by collaborating, communicating, learning rules, and supporting each other. But the idea that winning isn't everything, it's the *only* thing—that is the problem. It paves the way for athletes to accept aggressive behavior from their fellow athletes or their coaches.

Have you ever really listened to how some coaches speak to their athletes to motivate or inspire them? Shouting, name calling, aggression, shaming—these words and behaviors would be considered abusive in any other environment, and likely get us fired. Does a culture that steps out of the bounds of acceptable interpersonal behavior really build champions? Or does it make mental health harder to maintain? Does it encourage risk-taking or exploitative behavior, convince athletes that the rules apply only to other people, and teach aggression, manipulation, and emotional abuse?

I know the answer, and I work to examine this process and *recreate* a culture of champions by developing a culture of care. The first step is to create an environment of psychological safety and security. We do this by developing trust within our organizations, for all teammates, coaches, and athletes, to help them learn how to strive for success instead of fear failure. Psychological safety starts with identifying and understanding the culture we strive to build; naming it, defining its value, and prioritizing our need for it, because culture creation for champions begins with *caring*. It means caring for the people we work *with*, the people we work *for*, and caring for the mission we're going to live by.

It absolutely means caring about and striving for wins and championships. But first it means caring about the culture that allows championships to happen when a culture of care is really embraced. Winning becomes an outcome of a shared investment in our values, a shared consciousness in the behaviors we expect from everyone, and a shared commitment to the outcomes we're building our culture for.

Yes, this lofty goal requires a lot of communication. Real transformation takes time and dedication. It demands that we invest in showing our vulnerability. As we begin to connect with each other this way, we can identify what values we need to build a secure environment that will maximize the extraordinary skills and passion of our athletes and everyone who works to support them.

The intangible work of creating a psychologically secure environment happens when we set an emotional tone for an organization and build awareness of emotional regulation—our ability to effectively manage and respond to emotional experiences—in *every* team member, coach, and leader. Sport is emotional. Stress, anxiety, anger, sadness, shame, and frustration are all natural consequences of working toward championships. Learning to understand these ups and downs and channel the tremendous energy created in athletics can fuel a culture of care where people can thrive.

When we learn how to turn the emotion up or down like a thermostat, we can control the healthy homeostasis of the culture. We achieve this through several teachable skills. First, cultures of care value and encourage feedback at every level of an organization. It can be hard to summon the courage to ask for feedback and receive it with confidence. Psychologically secure and safe organizations offer—and receive— constructive feedback with compassion, not defensiveness or destructive criticism. We often think of feedback as only negative, but it's not. It's paying attention to how the people in our environment feel, and how they're showing their feelings. Validation and praise are important components. When we acknowledge the good work of others, we create a culture of care by reinforcing acceptance, praise and mutual support.

We build our team by seeing, hearing, and understanding each other. By sharing our knowledge in the process of communicating, offering feedback, and receiving it. This shared knowledge allows everyone to do their job as well as possible. It reinforces individual security and confirms that they have the information and support they need without having to stress about mind reading or guessing at someone else's thoughts or intentions.

Step two is to educate our coaches. Coaches are so impactful to every athlete, their support staff, and set the cultural tone of the organization. The role of a coach carries tremendous weight—a weight we often don't fully acknowledge. Most coaches don't want to harm their athletes, they aim to be positive role models for them. But that's not always how it works.

People perceive coaches as the only person with *all* the answers, the source of *all* technical methodology of play, the wizard behind the curtain, and the final decision maker. This role carries enormous responsibility, and the burden for an entire team's success, but we often forget the emotional load this requires them to carry. It's a heavy one. Coaches tend to the emotional needs of players, juggling dozens of personalities and different communication styles and levels of emotional intelligence at once. Teaching coaches how to set an effective emotional tone, to motivate, to care, to encourage, and to give hard feedback contributes to a psychologically safe and secure culture of care.

Naturally, healthy communication is the most important component to building a culture that minimizes harm while surfacing the greatest capabilities in each person. It can be challenging to re-learn communication, but it is worth the effort. The outcome changes environments from silent and anxious to open, more compassionate, mutually supportive, healthier, and better able to solve problems. To environments that banish shame and silence. Communication reduces the potential for harm that can come from heightened emotions. It lowers the stress and pressure of performance-based organizations, like every team in sport everywhere. Ultimately athletes in these environments are more capable of winning championships. They're stronger than their competitors because they have the secret superpower of care.

The intangible capabilities that define the mental and emotional skills of a team or organization can make the difference between good and great cultures. Even though we can't always see them, we know they exist. We feel them.

They're the emotional heartbeat and energy in a room. They inspire us to be our best selves. They're how we instill greatness. They start with a belief in the importance of an integrative approach to championship building which integrates mental, physical, and emotional training. No one of these components is more important than any other. They all need to be learned, performed, and cared for in recovery processes that build every champion and championship team.

SIXTEEN

Addressing Trauma on Our Teams: Rebuilding Sport Culture into a Culture of Care

Our culture of winning *at all costs* creates a culture of trauma for athletes and means losing when a win may have been possible. This is another opportunity where coaches and organizational leaders can have an outsized impact. As they learn to lead as part of a culture of care that values psychological safety and security, their ability in coaching athletes to develop life skills that help prevent traumatic experiences, and heal from them, also grows and deepens.

There are a few core skills that help to chip away at the "winning at all costs" mentality. These are *goal setting, coping, communication, time management, leadership,* and *problem solving.* Most important in these life skills seems the simplest, but it's not. Coaches and athletes need to relearn how to actually *feel their feelings.* So much of our environment tells us not to feel, but to bury our universal emotions, as I did at age nine before the biggest and scariest race of my life.

Instead of masking our emotions, we can learn how to use them to facilitate our performance. Strengthening our emotional muscles makes the whole human stronger. This assists us in life if trauma happens again by making us better able to respond. Think of it as a form of mental health training, but of the emotional kind.

Imagine if we started teaching emotional awareness with as much attention as we pay to our physical health. Think about what would be possible if we started to understand that we have six universal emotions that everyone on earth experiences—sadness, anger, happiness, joy, disgust, and fear—and we're all feeling many of them, a lot of the time. Building a culture of care and a psychologically safe place in sport means understanding that we are all subject to these universal emotions, that we can safely explore them in ourselves and understand them in others.

Until we shift our culture of sport and reframe it from *only* championship building, we're not going to reverse the tide of mental health challenges facing athletes, at any level of competition, and we're not going to be able to fix what's wrong in the culture of sport. Beyond missing the opportunity to create environments that give rise to the highest level of athletic performance, we're maintaining a culture that casually promotes harm, even if it's unintentional. We don't talk about what we should do differently. We don't really examine how we got here. We tolerate the bracketed morality that spills out beyond our teams and into the rest of our lives.

Failing to reexamine our culture perpetuates the extreme importance we place on a player's athletic identity to the detriment of everything else. It also tells athletes that their identity—as a champion—has an expiration date, and without it they have very little to contribute. What happens when athletic careers end, either abruptly and prematurely because of an injury, or even in an ideal retirement, after a long and successful career?

Thousands of athletes leave competition every year without a sense of who they are outside of the bright light of attention their skills brought them. Finding the new facets of ourselves can be a very difficult path, and without the benefits of a culture of care, sport sets them up for the rude awakening of trying to reorient their identity alone. This may set them up for failure in their post-sport life, as the toxic culture continues to affect them. The prohibition to feel their feelings, silence their anxieties or depression, and ignore the unexamined emotional problems they carry won't go away.

A culture of care teaches the skills to manage this change in identity, helping to relieve the pressure from the mandate to appear strong and invincible. After the championships are long over, with bodies that bear the wounds of competition, our athletes may fall further into poor mental health. All of life's emotional issues can take center stage, and there may be decades ahead of dealing with the aftermath of the stress, anxiety, and depression athleticism can lead to. This is a lot to handle; and most people do it silently, without the strengthened skills to overcome these issues.

We can help prepare them for tomorrow by protecting them today, as we develop a culture of care that teaches them how to change their thoughts from sport being what and who they *are*, to what they *do*. There is life after sport. If we make the culture of sport more complete, we have the power to impact every stage of an athlete's life through an environment that connects the body, the mind, and the feelings we all carry.

Our feelings are the gateway to our connections. People who feel more connected to others have lower levels of anxiety and depression, have higher levels of self-esteem and empathy for others, and are more trusting and cooperative. As a consequence of all these good things, these people are more mentally healthy, and connection is the foundation of mental health.

This is the most foundational building block of who we are—we seek connections. Nowhere is that more evident than on our teams, whether we're doing it consciously or not. We're social beings and we need to be together with others. It's a part of our adaptive toolkit. It allows us to do things we wouldn't be able to do on our own—like win championships—which is why team connections are so strong.

But our mental health is constantly challenged because people don't feel comfortable relating to how they really feel. While we may be among people every day, we're leaning very hard into our quiet individualism and away from our collective group mentality. We all do it. We shy away from our own feelings that make us uncomfortable. We bury the problems and pain in our lives so deeply that we can barely access them in ourselves, making us even more remote and inaccessible. This is the opposite of working toward a culture of care and ensuring psychological safety and security.

Our language is partly to blame. When was the last time you asked someone how they were, hoping to hear nothing more than "Fine"? We all do it, but why? Is it because we don't want to actually relate to the person when we are asking? Is it easier or safer for us to answer "Good," fulfilling the unspoken mandate to always be in top form, never weak, sad. or angry, just "fine"? The truth is, we don't have the time or inclination to be honest. This lack of honesty robs us of the opportunity to create real connections and unload some of what is the hardest for us to carry alone.

For traumatized people within organizations that aren't leading with care, this only leads to silence.

This shorthand has made dealing with trauma much harder. For many of us, our natural inclination to tell someone how we're really feeling is curbed by the knowledge that they're just going through the motions of being polite. This is part of our natural process of growing up and being socialized, in which we learn to suppress how we really feel. At some point, we learn that other people can't or won't connect with our real feelings, so we push them down in order to reduce the friction in our lives. It's inauthentic and leaves suppressed emotion all around us, just beneath the surface.

These unprocessed emotions make us feel blank, numb, nervous, stressed, and anxious, though we're not sure why. Emotional repression in ourselves leads to a sense of unease and discomfort when *other* people express their emotions. And we're all doing it, whether we realize it or not.

We can't handle holding our own emotions let alone attempt to handle other people's feelings. More often than not, we don't want them, can't take them on, and can't deal with them when they surface around us. Sometimes, because feelings have been trapped for so long, they emerge in floods of tears, anger, or pain, and we recoil from the outburst. This coping mechanism is damaging everyone. Without a culture of care, we lose emotional regulation, as we rarely uncork the bottle enough to let out how we really feel. The pressure builds to dangerous levels. We see this all over the culture of sport, not only in headlines, but from the sidelines of our children's athletic events.

There is real danger in how we've made the honest expression of normal feelings unwelcome in our environment. But I also see a place to make massive changes across the culture of sport. In our personal lives, at work, and in athletics, we have the space and skills to prioritize making this change. A place where we can actually feel our feelings and express them in healthy ways before we explode outwardly and cause trauma in others. This is where preventive mental health care enters our culture. It's how we can change the destructive culture of emotional silence in sport.

Think about it like this: any emotional spike from someone else—a teammate, a coach—confronts our own repressed feelings. It reminds us of the mess we carry under the surface and challenges our ability to cope. What if we could let it all out in healthy ways? What if we had the skills to do this because we were part of a culture that trains and develops our bodies *and* our minds? Wouldn't we be healthier? We would be happier, that is guaranteed.

Constantly censoring ourselves and never allowing ourselves to be vulnerable means we can never *be* ourselves. And never being ourselves perpetuates our toxic culture that hides the trauma. This is depleting every resource we have, stressing our bodies in dangerous ways, and leaving us unprepared to confront any difficult situation that arises in life. There is no way to live a life without some emotional potholes, or even catastrophic sinkholes. But we aren't prepared. How can we be?

Professional athletes don't live a normal life compared to other people. Athletes are monitored and assessed more than anyone else as to what they eat and how they train; they're praised constantly while simultaneously being shamed for losing; they live in doubt and fear of failure; and there is constant pressure to hide any weakness, all while being watched by millions of people.

Think about how we have contributed to putting collegiate and professional athletes on a pedestal. We shower them with perks and special rules, while accepting bracketed morality for their off-the-field behavior. More and more, we invest in their material, championship-winning success. This turns sport into getting paid to play and eliminates many of the positive developmental aspects of athletics. For young athletes, we invest in their future championships, reaffirming their "win at all costs" value, while robbing them of the opportunity to develop mental health through athletics.

This *win at all cost* mindset happens when athletes are coached through fear. It exacerbates the pressure to perform and contributes to creating a culture that mandates one should remain silent about the trauma they may experience. It tells athletes that they're only good enough if they have the potential to contribute to a win. Fear, shame, disappointment, and reduced enjoyment bleeds through the sacrifices these champions make in the hope of being among the 1% that make it to the next level. Then, if they do make it to the next level, the high-pressure petri-dish of sport culture's champion mindset only grows stronger—spreading more fear of failure, fear of evaluation, and fear of not being good enough that brews inside hopeful champions.

Simultaneously, this mindset feeds the egos of those who are winning. It fuels the egos of coaches, parents, and organizational leaders who pay for these systems in the hope of creating championship cultures. But the cultures are missing out on the *person* within the player who is giving everything they have to perform for the rest of us. The person, the player, and the human within can't fully thrive within sport culture as it is today, because we haven't focused on building a culture of care.

Sport can change this, and the needs of our athletes demand that they get this chance. The system that creates champions and wins championships has room for this. We just need to prioritize it and make it our standard, our values, and our goal. We have the power to nurture healthy connections, not support the fearful avoidance that is the current standard. Digging into discomfort isn't easy, but there's no other way to clear the air to develop a culture of care.

SEVENTEEN

Our Team Values Matter

Like so many other things—and so many bad things—happiness and health are contagious. We impact one another every single day, and if we silence ourselves, we see more silence around us. But if we live authentically, honestly, and vulnerably, we create space for others to do the same. These positive emotions are transmitted through each of us, and being good to others is good for us too. As we show connection and care for people around us it spreads through every environment we pass through.

Treating other people with care isn't just a standard to live by. It boosts our mental and physical health. Small gestures have a big impact, and they don't just make the world a better place. They boost feelings of confidence, being in control, happiness, and optimism. Acts of kindness and care encourage others to pay forward the good deeds they've experienced, which slowly but surely contributes to a more positive, connected, healthier organization and team. This works quickly within teams especially, as it becomes the standard, the values shared by people who work together to support each other.

The core values of care—being warm, open, and generous with our time for each other—require courage and strength, but it helps us as much as it helps others. Our willingness to celebrate other people and focus the attention outside ourselves boosts our mood and lowers our stress levels. We can connect with more empathetic engagement. We can make more time for people, we can listen more actively, and we can show we understand each other. These are the foundations of care. This isn't altruism; it's our humanity and it makes teams and organizations unstoppable.

These seemingly small moments or acts that deepen connection with others affect our sense of satisfaction in our own lives, increase our self-esteem, and strengthen our empathy muscles. They decrease our blood pressure and reduce cortisol, which work together to directly lower our stress levels. Kindness positively changes our brains. As we're rewarded with more joy and happiness, it becomes contagious in communities.

If it seems like a far stretch for an athletic, high-performing environment to instill this value at its core you wouldn't be wrong. But why let that stop us? Why not begin to shift your mindset into an act of creating a culture of care and reducing the harm created within the walls of high-performance domains.

Real care is a form of intelligence, and cultures that prioritize this value are more successful. The foundation of a healthy brain is connection. It requires us to think not only about ourselves, but about who is around us. It requires the ability to reason and develop situational awareness in which we see others' distress or verbally unexpressed emotions. This allows us to feel, see, and understand the trauma in other people, which is the foundation of our empathetic connections. If we don't make these changes and get to the most honest and vulnerable place of seeing people's pain, then we're causing more harm and continuing our culture of silence about trauma.

We can achieve a culture change in sport to being open, empathetic, and aware of how other people feel. This is the antidote to the aggression and bracketed morality that is sidelining our athletes' mental health. It is a perspective shift to focus on enhancing mental health, psychological safety, and security in our culture. It demands that we be responsive and open, and that we engage with people intentionally, in spite of how scary that can be. Care depends on vulnerability and communication, even if we feel anxious or stressed at the thought of taking in someone else's feelings.

Our emotional superstructure—our morals and values, how we show up in the world, how we care for others—is who we are. It's what people will remember about us after we're gone, and it's the first thing we notice about someone new. It's the essence of each of us. We take it with us everywhere we go and we leave some of it behind in how we treat people.

As much as care can positively impact anywhere a kind person goes, the impact left behind by trauma has the opposite effect. Care confers humanity, but trauma, and traumatic experiences that are poorly worked through within people or organizations, leave a lasting scar.

There is a ripple effect when a response to trauma within an organization lacks empathy or trust. The harm is amplified, and the message is clear: no one is safe here. Most organizations miss the mark when responding to a traumatic experience that affects everyone. They lean into legalese and ignore the emotional connections people have with each other and with their workplaces. Official responses are often reactionary, in an effort to gain control over a situation and quiet any chatter. Everything is buried. But those in charge of the response rarely think through the emotional impact that's happening. They miss opportunities to be transparent, which deepens distrust within the organization and maintains the status quo of a toxic culture.

After a traumatic or stressful event on a team, a clear action plan is rarely communicated from the top that assures people they are safe and will be protected and explains what will be done to right a wrong. Without this, how can anyone feel safe in an environment where trauma occurred? It virtually guarantees that no one else will come forward, having seen how botched the first response was. Keeping silent and ignoring the problem becomes the norm.

Psychologically safe workplaces don't punish or humiliate people for speaking up, asking questions, communicating concerns, or calling out dangerous behavior. Instead, they make space for these needs. They make clear that bad behavior won't be tolerated or ignored. When people don't feel safe speaking up the risks of harm grow exponentially. However, in cultures that don't silence people who want to communicate honestly, authentically, and vulnerably to make positive change, the care factor sets the standard of excellence. In these environments, the expectation of care means everyone can be completely transparent. They can act when needed, with empathy and responsibility to do the right thing: show up for people who need help, care for everyone, and maintain a standard of safety and security.

In sport, we can create more cultures of care and accountability. Developing and maintaining safety on a team is a group effort, which means athletic organizations should make this a focus of their energy. Unless this is prioritized, nothing happens, and people get hurt. Once they're hurt, the support that doesn't come hurts even more. Broken communication leads to more harm done. More harm done further degrades how organizations treat the people who choose to devote their energy, passion, and expertise to the collective effort of creating winning cultures.

Sport organizations often respond to disruptive or traumatic events by doing nothing. This inaction highlights the disconnect between the values teams aspire to embrace and the values they actually live by. Instead of talking about values, we can *be* about these values. It starts with the coaches and leaders who can create a culture of care for a culture of champions. But it takes more than words painted on a wall. It requires actions in the hallways where our teams connect with and support one another.

Even the process of joining a new athletic organization is disjointed. It nearly always means being thrown into the fire of meeting dozens of new faces and struggling to remember their names and roles, with a glaring omission: who to speak with and what to do if something goes wrong. All while trying to do the best job they're capable of.

Rare is the organization that prioritizes psychologically safe environments. Instead of offering continuous learning opportunities or creating time and space for real, honest, vulnerable conversations about what it feels like to work there, everyone is laser focused on performance and delivering the best work they can. It's difficult to ask for help or raise a concern that threatens their security.

This sets up the employee for total failure. There is no space for prevention and psychological safety, only reactiveness after the fact. There is no opportunity to check in regularly with the leaders who have the power to enact change. There is only time for getting on with it and getting work done.

What's missing here? Trust.

Trust is the foundation of how we can create psychological safety and security. It is the core of a culture of care. Without trust and a belief in the other values of our teams, there is no shared purpose and no sense of mutual respect. Guess where that leads? To silence.

No one can have faith that the anxious feeling they get from a colleague or an act of aggression will be properly handled. So, they give up, try to protect themselves, and shut down. They internalize the pain and cycle through feelings of anxiety, stress, apathy, and the fear of walking back into work. People stop caring, and they disengage from the shared purpose. It weakens rather than strengthens the team and the culture of sport.

All of this shutting down and silencing our instincts to ask for help, seek safety, and connect with others in times of trouble is damaging how we show up for what we do. It makes many people feel out of control. No one can thrive in the mixed message of "Show up as your best self, do your best work, and make this organization as successful as it can be, while burying how you really feel, what is happening to you, and the harm we're doing. But work harder, because you're lucky to be here. Walk on eggshells and say nothing, because saying nothing is easier than speaking up. Don't draw attention to yourself." We rationalize our thoughts and accept the negative feelings and unhealthy environment because it is our duty to serve, to aid in the chase for championships.

This doesn't make sense and it isn't living sport's highest values. It doesn't develop people into healthy champions; it damages people. We can do better. Let's treat our people as our greatest asset and the team, reputation, or the output of our work as a secondary consequence of creating the best and safest workplace possible. Let's live our values and promote the developmental aspects of sport, which teaches teamwork and mutual support and pulls the best out of people. Let's work together to win championships. We all want to contribute our best work. We want to connect on a more authentic level, so we can live our purpose. Our purpose goes beyond winning. It's about *how* we win.

EIGHTEEN

The Time Is Now to Change Our Culture

There's a sense of power and security for an athlete that comes from knowing what their team stands for, and living their highest values of truth, honesty, transparency, and strength in the face of a challenge or conflict. Yes, bad things happen on teams. People show bad judgment, harass, intimidate, and attack others. They let their emotional dysregulation seep out and people get hurt. We can't control all the ways people can be harmful to others. But the key to healing these problems in sport is by living our highest values. Our team gets stronger and is more able to withstand problems, because our values are always front and center. Our connections are at the core of our values. When we know what we stand for, these connections flourish.

Connection with other people is an investment we make. We all do it, though we're barely conscious that we're growing something.

Every time we connect honestly with someone, we're investing more of ourselves into others, believing it will pay off. This is hopeful and vulnerable and so human. It's what keeps us all going, and it's how every team operates. The payoff from our human investments is learning emotional regulation and forging deeper connections as we listen and use emotional language to speak. We invest more of ourselves. Teams in sport are defined and bound together winning and losing as a group, training, growing, and learning incrementally. But the foundation of what it means to be part of the team are the connections.

When trauma is an invisible teammate, it transmits through our connections, and makes investing in the team harder. It creates issues that hinder team growth and success. As sport organizations focus on healing the issues that arise, leaders can be stewards of the connections and investments their team members make in one another. The work to heal starts with leadership.

The first step for a sport organization to heal is through the process of *empathetic engagement*. This is an open, transparent conversation about events that occurred where any kind of pain was an outcome for any team member or the organization as a whole. It creates space for anyone and everyone to name, feel, lean in, and learn. It allows people to speak openly and express their feelings and concerns. It makes space for complicated emotions and varied responses to obstacles and issues facing the team and the organization. Empathetic engagement helps the invisible teammate, trauma, to be seen, held, and carried not only by the individual but by any member of the organization.

Beginning with empathetic engagement is not only addressing harmful events in a candid, vulnerable way. It's a form of *harm reduction*. It communicates that the problem is not being ignored, minimized, or hidden. Instead, it's being laid bare to be processed and learned from so it can't harm anyone in silence.

Many organizations don't know where to start. Empathetic engagement begins with a framework to deal with the complicated issues that impact the health, well-being, and sense of safety of a team.

1. Acknowledge that something happened.
2. Seek feedback, consult with experts if action or resources are needed from outside the organization, and follow their guidance.
3. Conduct conversations with care with everyone involved.
4. Ask what people may need—including outside resources, time, or space or more time to talk.
5. Provide a plan of action, together, with a time frame.
6. Openly discuss the action steps and start to implement them.
7. Have more check-in conversations with care with any and all team members involved, in groups, privately, or both.

This process takes time, intention, attention, and the ability to really listen. Some people will know how they feel and have immediate responses. Others will need time to process and understand their own thoughts and feelings before being able to communicate them. Everyone processes information on a different schedule. Part of the value of seeking feedback and conducting several check-in conversations is that team members are allowed to come forward when they're ready.

Healing within this framework can happen on an individual level, in small groups, or collectively as a community. Think about sending emails that keep everyone included, holding town hall meetings, or offering educational webinars. But whatever form this communication takes, leaders need to guide the process.

Teams want and need leaders to lead. Not only in response to an event or bad experience, but in anticipation of and preparation for an intervention when it does. Leaders must hold people at all levels accountable for their actions. And when trauma does happen, leaders must use empathetic engagement, which means addressing it, always.

A proper response to trauma is not achieved by taking a one-and-done, cover-up approach. Healing requires ongoing care and attention. The lessons learned from reflective sharing and open communication after an event are essential. Leaders need to create space to reflect, respond, and communicate. Dealing with or managing traumatic events means accountable action. Only empathetic engagement and accountability can help organizations improve and heal from traumatic events These lessons can become part of a team's core values, so when something else occurs, the muscles of empathetic engagement are already strengthened and individuals within the organization are better prepared to respond.

Through the process of empathetic engagement, our teams can learn how to heal, treat, and rehab any emotional wound. It will take time, attention, and care for teams to work with the invisible teammate among us—trauma—and manage the destructive impact trauma has on individuals and organizations. Let's face it, there will always be more of it. We need to examine where it is and how it operates and find ways to work *with* it, rather than *against* it. The invisible teammate of trauma isn't going anywhere. While we may not want it on our team, we must come to terms with it, learn to grow from it, and use its impact to strengthen us.

When unexpected events occur, we are most inspired by teams that name and address the situation quickly. It communicates to everyone that their values are consistent with a caring culture. These are based on the best practices of taking care of people *within* an organization, so the organization can be its best self internally and externally.

Teams that respond and hold people accountable aren't afraid of issues that arise. They don't sweep things under the rug. They shine a light on them. These actions say they're empathetic first—because they care about humans—and compassionate, because they're working together as a team to name and face the facts. It's the highest standard of professional practice. The expectation that everyone is being held accountable creates a foundation of how we treat others.

Creating a culture of care names the feeling everyone is having, answers their unspoken questions, and normalizes the tone in the organization. It sets the framework for leaders to lead, protect their people, and create opportunities to succeed. Without this, though, people explode. They transmit their stress and anxiety everywhere. They guess at the facts, making any kind of truth-seeking harder, and they stop trusting the people leading them.

No one can deny an issue if leaders address it directly, and no one can pretend it's not worth their time and attention. When leaders speak, their teams listen, even if it's uncomfortable. And isn't it better to be uncomfortable in the truth than uneasy in silence and denial? Ignoring an issue creates an unsafe place where fear of judgment, shame, and retaliation thrive. The only way to cure this and minimize damage is to take ownership of the problem. It starts with the leaders and decision makers of a team and should become an established baseline of functioning for everyone within an organization. This shows every teammate that the truth matters, and they will be held to the same standard.

What we don't want is for our teams to talk about their values of safety, inclusion, and honesty, then fail to live up to them. We don't want the hypocrisy of talking about mutual respect while lying for someone or ignoring calls for help. We don't want anyone to pretend things will go away quietly—they never do—or become silent bystanders.

We want people to talk about their values and then put them into action. We want teams to speak up, be direct, delegate, and show up. Leaders and decision makers do not have easy jobs, but there are many words not heard often enough, and we can correct this. "I've made a mistake. We made an error in judgment. We will correct that misstep. I have your back. I understand your concerns, so let's pause while we work on addressing these issues." These may not always be the easiest things to say, but they go a long way to creating the culture of care that keeps everyone accountable and focused on the highest values of the organization.

Without them, though, we get siloed silence. This exists in places where the hierarchy becomes clear. When there's no more flat structure, there's no capacity to work together as an organization to be transparent. It means teams can't work together to build a culture of care. This guarantees that problems will multiply. And once they multiply, they can take control of any organization or team, overwhelming everyone's best efforts to maintain psychological safety and security.

No one can ask for help if they're fearful they'll be seen as weak, incompetent, and dumb. It takes a lot of security to seek help and support. In a psychologically unsafe environment, no one is secure enough to be honest about what they're experiencing. People become so afraid of communicating the *right* way, so they don't communicate at all. What if their ask for support is misinterpreted? What if they lack the emotional vocabulary to communicate what's wrong? What if they can't describe the help they need?

In these instances, leadership and decision makers are leaving their teams outside a culture of care and ignoring the safety and security needs of their teams. True leaders ask the right questions, check in with people, feel the vibe in their organization, and don't wait for issues to be brought to their attention. In psychologically unsafe places, people don't bring problems to leaders unless they have no other option, because the environment has told everyone that speaking up is unsafe. No one wants to share the truth and be transparent, because they have no faith that they will be supported up and down the organization.

Many leaders or coaches may respond to this by saying that they don't have time to check in with their teams on a level that creates consistency, promotes growth, and facilitates change. It makes sense. We coach how we were coached, lead how we were led. We live in cultures that were created for us and change often only occurs when it's going bad or ownership and leaders change. The reality is, we can be constantly growing, evolving, and checking in to ensure our highest standards and values are being lived. People make the culture, and people change, evolve, grow, and have different needs. Our cultures need to continuously evolve with the people who serve them.

At this point, championships don't matter, because winning becomes meaningless in a culture of fear and unlived values. It erases our humanity and corrodes what matters most: making space for people to thrive, be happy, healthy, and productive, and commit to teams that value them. How can anyone do their best and really deliver results in an environment like this? How can anyone feel safe?

They can't, and no one wants to. People will devote every shred of themselves to places where they feel seen, heard, and safe. They will thrive when they feel in control of how they can work and are free to speak their minds. They will have room to be honest and vulnerable in an environment that cares for them and protects them.

Ensuring psychological security starts with communication and grows from there. As we continue to examine how we work in sport we will be able to understand and change the restrictive emotional language we use. We will start to see the unnoticed, speak the unspeakable, and hear the unmentionable. When we shake our stale and unproductive norms, we can make work, connecting, and competing healthier for everyone.

NINETEEN

The Role of Leaders in a Culture of Care

I'm passionate about calling attention to the toxic culture of sport and creating a culture of care for a culture of champions, because I care deeply about who we are and what we value in sport. I've been an athlete, I work with athletes, and I'm raising athletes. I love this environment and I've been hurt in this environment, often. I'm hurt from personal experiences. I carry the hurt from the stories I get to hold as I aid others in healing. And I hurt from the stories I read and observe across the world of athletics.

I strive to be a leader in the space of a culture of care, and I do not want to just pay lip service to safety and security. It's more than my mantra; it represents the values I live by. I know we can all integrate it into what we do. I want our work to be authentic, honest, and transparent. Then we can support and care for our people and reduce the harm done by how much trauma operates silently within our culture. I want fighters. I want heart. And I am here to help those who are with me, who see it, feel it, and are as fed up with it as I am.

Many employees and leaders at every level aren't doing the work that is needed to create true psychologically safe and secure workplaces. This isn't just a value that's nice to have. It's a requirement for the health and well-being of everyone working for them. It's the way to win championships. It's how we create teams and organizations that live their highest values and share them with the world.

At their core, great organizations that are intentional about setting people up for long-term success live by an overarching cultural goal while also building every champion within to achieve that goal. Organizations that only focus on an individualistic "one person at a time, there are only a few stars here" approach miss the connectivity of the group. They're exclusive rather than inclusive. Organizations that only focus on the outcome and a championship path often forget those who are serving and building in smaller, less noticeable ways. When this happens, they will never get the best creative, confident, and innovative individuals to perform.

The real leaders doing the work to create a culture of care that builds champions within an overarching championship culture are serving everyone, even those whose skills are not part of the history of sport. It's much easier to create a culture of care and psychological safety and security than one may think. It happens simply by seeing our humanity first. Wins become a consequence of caring. Caring and supporting each other is the most important thing we have. We need it so much, not only because it's in such short supply, but because it's how we create *anything* at all. Every single human endeavor, every single team, every champion or championship is a consequence of how people connect, communicate, share, laugh, cry, struggle, fail, and succeed. Cultures are not words on a wall, cultures are not based only on championships won or lost. Cultures are not just built once. Cultures are built by the environment around them, the people within them.

Connection gives us the sense of belonging we need. It goes beyond respect and care to create a culture that focuses on the complete champion, not just the athlete who scores points and wins at all costs. Connection is how we heal. It's how we prevent pain and intervene when pain occurs. Healing leads to growth, acceptance, restoration, and renewed hope. It can happen when we remove ourselves from trauma or abuse, or when we can finally exist in a culture of care that allows what hurts us to come to the surface.

Healing our emotional wounds helps us become more resilient. It gets easier to make the cognitive decision to choose emotional strength. It's a commitment to persevere through the adversities in our lives. In sport, it's what we coach and train athletes to do physically. Being resilient means responding mindfully, adapting and problem solving in any situation, and coping mentally, emotionally, and physically to nearly anything that comes our way. Being resilient is a choice, both for individuals and for organizations. It means bending, where breaking is also a possibility.

The five core pillars of personal resilience are *self-awareness, mindfulness, self-care, positive relationships,* and *purpose*. This framework can also help organizations heal if they have been through trauma. We often think that someone is resilient because they've overcome hardship. But the truth is, it's possible to build resilience that helps prevent traumatic experiences before they become the kind of trauma that's difficult to process and heal from. Building resilience enables people and organizations—through empathetic engagement—to adapt to difficult or challenging experiences, to bounce back, and it reinforces core strengths and values, even if we don't always know they're there.

But resilient organizations don't merely bounce back after adversity. They often find new strengths and capabilities, growing and becoming *more* resilient after difficult experiences. Rising to new challenges leads to emerging with a revised and improved team self-image, as they discover the unexpected abilities within their connection that they hadn't seen before. This can shift and clarify a team's priorities as they remove what no longer fits and replace it with more meaningful goals, values, and aspirations. This renewed purpose can strengthen our resolve, making our teams even more resilient.

Optimal environments that build safety and security create a place of working toward resilience because they show that they're prepared to grow, learn, and adapt to changing circumstances. This is the heart of what sport is, what athletes train for, and what teams are doing. They're in a constant state of learning, improving, and pushing themselves beyond what is possible today to achieve greatness tomorrow.

They respond to failure and keep showing up, keep trying, keep hoping, and keep believing that anything is possible if they work hard enough and learn in the process. This is the humanity in sport. It's a championship mindset that embraces resilience. Without adversity—or losing from time to time—we aren't challenged and without challenges, we can't adapt. Without adaptation, we can't reset. Resetting is reflecting on who we are and what our culture of sport means. It's how we focus on changing what isn't working for optimum care, safety, security, and ultimately, the highest standard of mental health for everyone involved.

One of the most important parts of healing is keeping at it even though it's so hard and painful and can feel very lonely. It's important to believe that we *can* heal, so we can see where we're going. Without this hope, the finish line of feeling better keeps fading into the distance. Resilience is faith in our ability to heal, and hope is that healing will come if we can do the work to get there.

Healing means we can begin to see, feel, hear, and *be* again. We can begin to come back to life, choose to engage, choose to connect, take more risks, feel more at peace, and feel safe again. The world seems slower as we regain control over our emotional range. Our energy begins to increase, and we feel *better*. When we go back to the feeling of the scar, there's less anxiety using the area that was wounded. There are fewer reminders of the pain because we're not hiding our scars. We've actually moved on from masking it. It's a part of us, but we're not hyper focused on it and the impact it has on us. It's just there.

This is what learning to live and work with our invisible teammate looks like. The trauma may still be there, but it's now a strength, rather than a weakness.

CONCLUSION

As I listen to and reflect on stories of abuse, they share many common characteristics. What surfaces most often is the fact that there is a hero in each of these stories, but all too often the hero is also the victim. Coming forward and standing up for oneself is the most astonishing act of bravery. Yet we barely acknowledge this fact. This is especially true in sport.

Refusing to go quietly, asserting one's right to safety, and casting the antiseptic light of truth on trauma takes courage that people who haven't experienced trauma can barely imagine. What heroes do, that is so simple, and yet so rare, is follow their convictions and say "Stop. This is not right. This is not okay, and I won't stand by and do nothing." The hero in every story of wrongdoings may look different, but the commonality is always the same. They are shining a light on the goodness in people and on the value of safety. Their spotlight illuminates the most confusing and painful part of becoming victimized by someone, a group, or an organization. They're showing us that we are not alone. That we are not crazy, and that there is hope of being safe again. The hero shows up and helps to calm the chaos—even though it's not a comfortable role for a victim.

I take comfort in the fact that there is a hero within all of us, no matter how small we think our impact can be or how low our position. Sometimes we need someone to scream for us. Sometimes we need someone to scream beside us and sometimes we need someone to scream behind us, but all echo the same message: *Do the right thing*. This has to stop. Be better. Be accountable. Take action. Do not look away, allow your discomfort to dull your values, or let the system off the hook. Demand better, so we can all *be* better.

The good in humanity is what builds the hero and gives them the courage to use their voice and stand up for what's wrong. It's the strength of the soul that guides the voice of the hero and protector within us to take action. Millions of people experience some form of assault or trauma each year. Too often, apathy paves the road ahead of victims, as they try to advocate for themselves. Imagine if heroes were on each of our teams, standing up for people in pain.

If no one stands up to be the hero, what are we supposed to tell our kids? That an overwhelming number of people are too weak, too self-centered, and too cowardly to help them if they need it? That our humanity is broken, no one is coming to help, and they're on their own? What kind of world does that leave? In my mind, it's a landscape of expired humanity in which every single person is in it for themself. There's no community, no kinship, no collectivism, and no reason to care about what other people go through. That world leaves our invisible teammate —trauma—in charge.

I'm not willing to attach my name to that dystopian world. I'm the hero to some people, just as others have been for me. I'm grateful for my heroes who showed up for me, who spoke up, and stood up for the right thing. I'm grateful for them, and for the chance to be my own hero and the hero my daughters see when they look at me today.

We each have the power to reduce the trauma that surrounds us by keeping our eyes open for changes in the people around us—grief, pain, anger, sadness, or fear. Without our heroism, how are we going to continue to teach the impact of right and wrong? This is not some pie in the sky, unattainable standard that only some people can rise to. We all can, at every level of sport. All around us, the wrong thing is happening, sometimes daily. There's no doubt that power is unequally distributed, but we all possess the same capabilities to watch, listen, see, and respond to problems. There's no guarantee that the right thing will happen. But can't we be sure that the wrong thing is guaranteed if no one does anything?

There's more to this idea of every person having hero potential than meets the eye. The impact of speaking out empowers others to do the same. It disempowers the toxic environments ruled by silence and a mentality of every-person-for-themself. And it allows space for other heroes to make some noise. A toxic environment, relationship, or dynamic can't survive if enough people speak up and agitate for change. Denial can't continue if enough courageous people refuse to play the game and choose to live by their values instead. We can't *all* be silenced if enough of us are willing to take the risks that come with refusing to accept what is "wrong" and making space for what's "right."

There is potential to force unsafe organizations to reform their toxic cultures so that routine harm to people is the exception and not the norm. These sport teams and organizations will not be able to function if a collective standard of security, honesty, and support is the mandate. But to do this requires the courage of millions of people willing to speak and show up for each other. It will take work to live by these values, but it's totally within our reach. Let's call it like we see it and accept the consequences, because when enough of us are willing to do something, everything changes.

Sport has the power to inspire and unite people in a way few other things can. It speaks to our deepest human needs for connection and belonging. We feel the highest highs and the lowest lows participating, devoting ourselves to our teams, and working to become champions who carry the aspirations of fans with them. My hope is that in the future, "It's been resolved" will mean something entirely different. It will happen when we live and work by a culture of care in sport that sees, hears, and addresses our traumas head on, and works actively to prevent harm. It will mean resolved on *our* terms, how *we* need it to be, without the weight of silence it imposes on victims of trauma today.

This will make a wrong right and will have the power to instill the kind of hope that helps heal our trauma.

REFERENCES

Merkel D. L. (2013). Youth sport: positive and negative impact on young athletes. *Open access journal of sports medicine, 4,* 151–160. https://doi.org/10.2147/OAJSM.S33556

McMillan, B. (2022, November 4). *Mental health and athletes.* Athletes for Hope. https://www.athletesforhope.org/2019/05/mental-health-and-athletes/

National Council for Behavioral Health. (n.d.). How to manage trauma—National Council for Mental Wellbeing. https://www.thenationalcouncil.org/wp-content/uploads/2022/02/Trauma-infographic.pdf

National Statistic Resource Center. (2015). *Statistics About Sexual Violence.*

U.S. Department of Health and Human Services. (2023, March). *Mental illness.* National Institute of Mental Health. https://www.nimh.nih.gov/health/statistics/mental-illness

Vernor, D. (2019, October 8). *PTSD is more likely in women than men*. NAMI. https://www.nami.org/Blogs/NAMI-Blog/October-2019/PTSD-is-More-Likely-in-Women-Than-Men

ABOUT THE AUTHOR

A clinical sport psychologist based in Austin, Texas, Dr. Hillary Cauthen was a Division 1 college track athlete, before embarking on a career focusing on the mental health and mental performance dimensions of athletes. She has developed private businesses that focus on mental wellness, performance optimization, and cultural well-being.